THE HUNT FOR PANCHO VILLA

The Columbus Raid and Pershing's Punitive Expedition 1916–17

ALEJANDRO M. DE QUESADA

First published in Great Britain in 2012 by Osprey Publishing
PO Box 883, Oxford, OX1 9PL, UK
1385 Broadway, 5th Floor, New York, NY 10018, USA
Email: info@ospreypublishing.com

Osprey Publishing is part of Bloomsbury Publishing Plc

Transferred to digital print on demand 2017.

First published 2012
2nd impression 2012

Printed and bound by PrintOnDemand-Worldwide.com, Peterborough, UK.

A CIP catalogue record for this book is available from the British Library.

Print ISBN: 978 1 84908 568 7
PDF e-book ISBN: 978 1 84908 569 4
EPUB e-book ISBN: 978 1 78096 049 4

Page layout by bounford.com, Cambridge, UK
Index by Sandra Shotter
Typeset in Sabon
Maps by bounford.com
Illustrated by Peter Dennis, Donato Spedaliere, Johnny Shumate
Originated by United Graphics Pte., Singapore

Acknowledgements
The Author would like to thank the following individuals, archives, museums, and societies:
Alex Mares (Interim Manager) and John Reed (Heritage Educator), Pancho Villa State Park;
Columbus N.M. Historical Society; Terry Hooker; Phillip Jowett; Douglas C. Dildy;
Bill Rakocy; Richard Dean; El Archivo Histórico de Ciudad Juárez; New Mexico State
University Library, Archives, and Special Collections Department, El Paso County
Historical Society; El Paso Museum of History; Fort Bliss Museum; and The Company
of Military Historians.

The Woodland Trust
Osprey Publishing are supporting the Woodland Trust, the UK's leading woodland
conservation charity, by funding the dedication of trees.

www.ospreypublishing.com

CONTENTS

INTRODUCTION

General Álvaro Obregón, General Francisco Villa Arámbula, and General John J. Pershing on the International Bridge between Ciudad Juárez and El Paso on August 27, 1914. Within two years after this meeting Pershing would be chasing Villa across northern Mexico. Of interest is the 2nd lieutenant standing behind Pershing – a very young George S. Patton. (AdeQ Historical Archives)

The Mexican Revolution for many conveys images of colorful figures – both hero and villain – as well as materials for popular culture and history. Numerous songs and films have used the revolution as its theme or even as a background to the main story. Of all the notables who made their niche in history, especially during the revolution, the most famous is Pancho Villa. For some he was a hero and military genius while for others he was little more than an opportunistic common criminal. In truth, he was somewhere between the two.

The motives behind Villa's raid on a small border town within United States territory have long been debated. This one raid would doom Villa and his men, even as it established them as a force to be reckoned with. In his shadow grew another star that would eventually outshine Villa. General John J. Pershing's Punitive Expedition, which was a result of the Villista Raid, would propel the United States into a campaign that would prepare the nation for an even greater conflict being fought in Europe at the time.

While the history of the Mexican Revolution definitely requires a larger volume, the purpose of this work is to primarily serve as a study of the raid on Columbus, New Mexico, and the subsequent Punitive Expedition.

ORIGINS

A Revolution South of the Border

The Mexican Revolution began in 1910 with an uprising led by Francisco I. Madero against longtime autocrat Porfirio Díaz. Several socialist, liberal, anarchist, populist, and agrarianist movements characterized the revolution, which changed over time from a revolt against the established order to a multi-sided civil war, The revolution created both heroes and villains throughout that bloody decade, among them a veritable *caudillo* of the northern Mexican state of Chihuahua.

José Doroteo Arango Arámbula, better known as Francisco "Pancho" Villa, came from the northern state of Durango. Villa with his army of Villistas joined the ranks of the Madero supporters. He led the Villistas in many battles, such as the attack of Ciudad Juárez in 1911 (which overthrew Porfirio Díaz and gave Madero a little power).

In 1911 Victoriano Huerta appointed Villa his chief military commander, but over the course of this appointment, Huerta and Villa became rivals. In 1912, when Villa's men seized a horse and Villa decided to keep it for himself, Huerta ordered Villa's execution for insubordination. Raúl Madero, brother of President Madero, intervened to save Villa's life. Jailed in Mexico City, Villa escaped to the United States. Soon after the assassination of President Madero, Villa returned with a group of companions to fight Huerta, whose plotting had seen him ascend to the presidency. By 1913 the group had become Villa's División del Norte (Northern Division), and included numerous American members. Villa and his army, along with fellow revolutionaries Venustiano Carranza and Álvaro Obregón, joined in resistance to the Huerta dictatorship.

Villa became provisional governor of the state of Chihuahua in 1914, and continued to receive international recognition: his tactics were studied by the United States Army and a contract with Hollywood was signed. By the terms of this agreement, Hollywood would be allowed to film Villa's movements and fifty percent of the profit would be paid to Villa to support the revolution. As governor of Chihuahua, Villa raised more money for a

1910

Start of the Mexican Revolution

drive to the south by printing his own currency. He decreed his paper money be traded and accepted at par with gold Mexican pesos, then forced the wealthy to give loans that would allow him to pay salaries to the army as well as supply them with food and clothes. He also took some of the land owned by the *hacendados* (owners of the haciendas) to give to the widows and family of dead revolutionaries. The forced loans would also support the war machinery of the Mexican Revolution. He confiscated gold from specific banks – in the case of the Banco Minero by holding hostage a member of the bank's owning family, the extremely wealthy Terrazas clan, until the location of the bank's hidden gold was revealed.

Villa's political stature at that time was so high that banks in El Paso, Texas, accepted his paper pesos at face value. His generalship drew enough admiration from the US military that he and Obregón were invited to Fort Bliss to meet Brigadier General John J. Pershing (1860–1948). The new wealth was used to purchase draft animals, cavalry horses, arms, ammunition, mobile hospital facilities (railroad cars and horse ambulances staffed with Mexican and foreign volunteer doctors, known as *servicio sanitario*), and food, as well as to rebuild the railroad south of Chihuahua City. This railroad transported Villa's troops and artillery south, where he defeated federal forces at Gómez Palacio, Torreón, and Zacatecas.

After Torreón, Carranza issued a puzzling order for Villa to break off action to the south and instead ordered him to divert to attack Saltillo, threatening to cut off Villa's coal supply if he did not comply. Coal was needed for railroad locomotives to pull trains transporting soldiers and supplies, so this was widely seen as an attempt by Carranza to divert Villa from a direct assault on Mexico City, allowing Carranza's forces under Álvaro Obregón, driving in from the west via Guadalajara, to take the capital first – and Obregón and Carranza did enter Mexico City ahead of Villa. This was an expensive and disruptive diversion for the División del Norte, since Villa's enlisted men were paid the then enormous sum of a peso per day, and each day of delay cost thousands of pesos. Villa did attack Saltillo as ordered, winning that battle.

Villa, disgusted by what he saw as egoism, tendered his resignation. Felipe Ángeles, one of Villa's chief advisors, and other members of his staff argued for Villa to withdraw his resignation, defy Carranza's orders, and proceed to attack Zacatecas, a strategic mountainous city considered nearly impregnable. Zacatecas was the source of much of Mexico's silver, and thus a supply of funds for whoever held it. Victory in Zacatecas would mean that Huerta's chances of holding the remainder of the country would be slim. Villa accepted Ángeles' advice, cancelled his resignation, and the División del Norte defeated the Federales in the Toma de Zacatecas (Taking of Zacatecas), the single bloodiest battle of the revolution, with the military forces counting approximately 7,000 dead and 5,000 wounded, and unknown numbers of civilian casualties. The loss of Zacatecas in June 1914 broke the back of the Huerta regime, and Huerta left for exile on July 15, 1914.

Huerta soon immediately plotted his return, however, traveling to Britain, then Spain, before returning to the States, landing in New York in 1915.

He made contact with supporters in exile in the US as well as with German agents and plotted to cross back into Mexico to retake power. Arrested in Newman, New Mexico, on June 27, 1915, he was charged with conspiracy to violate US neutrality laws and held in the US Army prison at Fort Bliss under house arrest due to risk of flight to Mexico. Huerta was an alcoholic and while in captivity he drank himself to death, dying in early 1916 in El Paso, Texas.

Villa and Carranza had different goals. Because Villa wanted to continue the revolution, he became an enemy of Carranza. After Carranza took control in 1914, the revolutionary *caudillos* held a National Convention, which set rules for Mexico's path toward democracy, and conducted a series of meetings in Aguascalientes. An interim president, Eulalio Gutierrez, was chosen; none of the armed revolutionaries were allowed to be nominated for government positions. Emiliano Zapata and Pancho Villa met at the convention, where Zapata told Villa he feared Carranza's intentions were those of a dictator and not of a democratic president. True to Zapata's prediction, Carranza decided to oppose the agreements of the National Convention, setting off a civil war. In the winter of 1914 Villa and Zapata's troops entered and occupied Mexico City. Villa's treatment of Gutiérrez and the citizenry outraged the more moderate elements of the population, who forced Villa from the city in early 1915.

The Conventionist forces under Pancho Villa were badly defeated by forces under the command of Álvaro Obregón, who supported the presidency of Venustiano Carranza, at the battle of Celaya Guanajuato on

The Villistas were adept in fighting through rough conditions whether on foot or on horseback. They are armed with 7mm Mexican Model 1910 Mausers. (AdeQ Historical Archives)

7

Major battles and border raids during the Mexican Revolution

April 13, 1915. Villa lost around 4,000 men killed in frontal attacks and had also lost an additional 1,000 horses, 5,000 rifles, and 32 cannons. Approximately 6,000 of his men were taken prisoner. Of those captured, 120 of Villa's officers were executed.

In this battle, Obregón developed a defense "in depth" that proved very effective against the offense-heavy cavalry charges and artillery techniques used at that time, and was based on his study of the trench conflict then raging in Europe. Although Obregón's lines weakened at times, he had sufficient reserves to bolster it at any point. Villa had committed all his men to the attack and was unable to exploit any area of weakness or to protect his flanks, which were enveloped by Obregón's cavalry.

The defending troops at Agua Prieta were led by Plutarco Calles and many of them were veterans who had already defeated Pancho Villa at the battle of Celaya earlier in the year. Calles, building on Álvaro Obregón's experience at Celaya, had erected extensive fortifications around the city, with deep trenches, barbed wire, and numerous machine-gun nests. Additionally, President Wilson gave permission for Carranzista troops to cross through US territory in order for them to be able to quickly strengthen the garrison at Agua Prieta. About 3,500 fresh veteran troops traveled through Arizona and New Mexico and arrived in the town in early October, bringing the total number of defenders to 6500. Villa was completely unaware of this development; according to the American correspondent and friend of Villa, John W. Roberts, Villa believed the town was defended by only 1200 soldiers.

Villa arrived at Agua Prieta on October 30, 1915, where, while giving his men a day of rest, he finally learned that the US had recognized Carranza, but not that they had also permitted his forces to cross American territory to strengthen the defenses of the town. As a result, Villa still believed that a swift cavalry charge, carried under the cover of darkness, was capable of capturing the city in one stroke. His staff officers believed that the town would be captured within five hours.

The next day Villa began his attack with an artillery barrage in the early afternoon, which only managed to detonate some of the land mines around the town that had been placed there by the Carranzistas. Once darkness had fallen he made some feints at various locations in order to hide the direction of his main attack. Shortly after midnight on November 2, he launched his frontal assaults from the east and south of Agua Prieta.

As the Villista cavalry was charging toward the trenches, however, two searchlights illuminated the battlefield, making the horsemen an easy target for Calles' machine guns. The front trenches were manned by units led by another future president of Mexico, Colonel Lázaro Cárdenas. Villa's horsemen were decimated by machine-gun fire and land mines, the few that managed to make it near the trenches encountering electrified barbed wire. The charge collapsed and the attack was a failure.

Pancho Villa wanted to continue with the cavalry charges on the following day; his troops, however, were ready to mutiny. He was also running low on supplies and ammunition. As a result, Villa withdrew and arrived at Naco,

Sonora, on November 4. Even though there his men were given rest, and supplies were acquired, more than 1,500 deserted from his army.

After resting his troops at Naco, Villa gathered up the remainder of his forces and attacked the town of Hermosillo, Sonora, on November 21, 1915. In order to try to restore the morale of his troops, Pancho promised them that after they took the city they could do whatever they wanted with the town and its inhabitants. This actually ended up causing the attack to fail, as his men almost immediately turned to looting and rape rather than fighting, which allowed the defending forces to reorganize and drive the Villistas out. Thereby, Villa's dominance in northern Mexico was broken in 1915 with the series of defeats he suffered at Celaya and Agua Prieta at the hands of Álvaro Obregón and Plutarco Elías Calles.

The División Del Norte

Pancho Villa's División del Norte initially began as 375 *vaqueros*, farmers, servants, orderlies, and rural peons who took up arms against the Mexican government. The men were originally organized into "columns" by Villa but as he gained combat field experience and as his army increased, more conventional units evolved. A total strength of 1,800 infantry, 2,800 cavalry, and 500 artillerymen with 36 guns existed in 1911. The following year the division was reorganized into three cavalry and four infantry brigades. By 1914 Villa's force included 40,000 men in 11 brigades with 60 guns in two regiments – effectively a corps-sized formation.

The División del Norte even had trains and an air arm. In March 1915 Villa's brother Hipolito arranged with Jack Berger, an entrepreneur who operated a traveling flying show, to supply Villa with planes and pilots. Berger purchased two airplanes from the Wright Factory – a Model B and a Model HS. They assembled the smaller Model B in Juarez, but before it could get off the ground a strong gust of wind blew it to pieces, injuring its pilot. The larger Model HS was hauled by train to Villa's headquarters in Monterrey. The train was painted a vivid green, and the name on the side of the cars read "Aviation Division of the North." Several test flights were made for Villa, who always came to watch but never went up. He did send an officer along though, in case the pilot decided to defect to Carranza. The plane's first mission, piloted by Howard Rinehart, was to carry orders to a regiment 50 miles to the south. On landing, he came under fire from Villa's own troops. The final mission for Rinehart was a message to troops in Matamoros. Rinehart later deserted from Villa's army and returned to Ohio. Americans mostly manned Villa's primitive air force. These pilots were ex-barnstormers and just as colorful as their comrades on the ground. They had names like Micky McQuire, Wild Bill Heath, and Farnum T. Fish.

Villa's defeats at the hands of his former allies destroyed his army in 1915 and by the following year only about 2,000 Villistas remained within the ranks. Villa briefly tried to rebuild his army using anti-American sentiments and Pershing's expedition as a rallying point but he was never able to gain the numbers he once had and his army melted away into the northern Mexican desert plains.

Villistas fighting in the streets of a northern Mexican town during the Mexican Revolution. A similar scene would have occurred in the streets of Columbus during that fateful morning of March 9, 1916. (AdeQ Historical Archives)

During this period Villa created an elite unit within the División del Norte. The Dorados, or the "Golden Ones," began life as a cavalry unit in late 1913 or early 1914. The unit provided him with an elite bodyguard throughout his military career and fought as shock troops in his battles. The Dorados were organized into three squadrons of 100 men, each man being provided with a rifle, two pistols, and two good horses. Many of the soldiers added gold trim to their hats as recognition of their elite status and in 1915 rode to their deaths against machine guns and artillery. By 1916 only about 50 were still in the saddle, including Julio Cárdenas, and those surviving Dorados remained loyal to Villa when he "retired."

America's First Intervention in Mexico

The revolution continued as in the United States a new American president, Woodrow Wilson, took office. Like its predecessor, the Wilson administration now faced the task of choosing a side in the ongoing Mexican Revolution. Wilson and his administration refused to recognize Huerta, because of the corrupt manner in which he had seized power, and it instituted an arms embargo on both sides of the civil war.

When Huerta's forces appeared to be winning the civil war in early 1914, Wilson lifted the embargo by offering to help Carranza. This action had volatile consequences. For several months, US Navy warships had been stationed at the ports of Tampico (under the command of Rear Adm. Henry T. Mayo) and Veracruz (under Rear Adm. Frank R. Fletcher's command) to protect American and other foreign interests associated with the rich oil fields in the area. On April 9, a group of sailors detached from the USS *Dolphin* went ashore at Tampico to retrieve supplies; Huerta's troops arrested and detained two of them. The sailors were released a short time later, and President Huerta offered an apology to the United States for the incident. Ultimately, Admiral Mayo demanded a 21-gun salute to the US flag in

Pancho Villa and his "Army of the North" on the move during the Mexican Revolution. (AdeQ Historical Archives)

addition to the apology. Huerta agreed only if the Americans would return the honor. When learning of the incident, an infuriated President Wilson refused Huerta's request Instead, he ordered the US Navy's Atlantic Fleet to Mexico's Gulf Coast to strengthen the forces under Mayo and Fletcher and occupy Tampico. Another crisis festering down the coast in Veracruz, however, prevented American troops from occupying the city, and the Tampico incident came to an end with no real conclusion.

The US consul's office in Veracruz had been warned that a German ship, the *Ypiranga*, delivering arms and military equipment for Huerta, was expected in the port on April 21, 1914. On the afternoon of 21 April, following orders from President Wilson, a contingent of 787 marines and sailors quickly went ashore and seized the customs house. By noon the following day, the US troops had occupied the town. Although they had hoped to avoid bloodshed, American forces were fired upon by Mexican soldiers and naval cadets, and a violent street battle ensued. The American losses were four killed and 20 wounded on 21 April, and 13 killed and 41 wounded on April 22. There is no accurate casualty number for the Mexican troops but it was reported by several sources that between 152 and 172 were killed and between 195 and 250 wounded. The German ship in question was diverted to another port and Huerta received the arms shipment after all.

On April 30, 1914, the US Army's Fifth Infantry Brigade, under the command of Brigadier General Frederick Funston, arrived at Veracruz. The brigade assumed occupation duty from the marines and also organized a

When US agents discovered that the German merchant ship *Ypiranga* was illegally carrying arms to the dictator Huerta, President Wilson ordered troops to the port of Veracruz to stop the ship from docking. The US did not declare war on Mexico but troops carried out a skirmish against Huerta's forces in Veracruz. The *Ypiranga* managed to dock at another port, which infuriated Wilson. On April 9, 1914, Mexican officials in the port of Tampico, Tamaulipas arrested a group of US sailors, including at least one taken from on board his ship and thus from US territory. After Mexico failed to apologize in the terms that the America had demanded, the US Navy bombarded the port of Veracruz and occupied the state for seven months. (AdeQ Historical Archives)

military government to restore order to the city. President Huerta never officially recognized the US occupiers but he made no serious attempts to resist their power. On July 15, 1914 Huerta resigned from the office of President and moved to Spain; American troops stayed on after his departure. That summer US military officers worked with the constitutionalist faction among the Mexican revolutionary forces in Veracruz, establishing a joint administration of the customs house and warehouse area. Between November 19 and 23, as the first American troops were leaving, US officers supervised the unloading from five ships of military materials, which filled the warehouses and piers. The Fifth Infantry Brigade left Veracruz on November 23, and the US government agreed that Carranza and his de facto government could use the city as their capital. Two months later, in their last act, the US officers turned over the warehouse keys to the constitutionalist leaders. When the forces of Venustiano Carranza marched out of Veracruz to defeat the other revolutionary factions, they carried a wide array of US-supplied arms.

German Intrigue in Mexico

The German drive to exert military influence in Mexico appears to have begun in 1900 with the arrival of Minister Edmund Freiherr von Heyking. Under Porfirio Díaz, the government was anxious to build a powerful Mexican army and to restrain the United States' influence, while the Germans were obviously only too glad to play one nation off against another and to gain what advantage they could in the process.

Carranza maintained Mexican neutrality throughout World War I. He briefly considered allying with the German Empire after German Foreign Secretary Arthur Zimmermann sent Mexico the famous Zimmermann Telegram in January 1917, inviting Mexico to enter the war on the German side. Zimmermann promised Mexico German aid in recapturing territory

Carranzistas, with a mixture of Mexican and American uniforms, equipment, and arms. The United States lent indirect support to the Carranzistas during the Mexican Revolution but relations between the two countries soured with Villista border excursions and the subsequent Punitive Expedition. (AdeQ Historical Archives)

lost to the United States during the Mexican–American War, specifically the states of Texas, New Mexico, and Arizona. Carranza assigned a general to study the possibility of recapturing this territory from the US, but ultimately concluded that it was not feasible.

This did not prevent Carranza accepting money and arms, or permitting German officers and soldiers serving as advisers of a German military mission to Mexico. An article in the *New York Times*, dated March 10, 1917, speculated on the number of German soldiers in Mexico:

As to the number of German army men in Mexico, it was said yesterday that there are at least 6,000 Germans in various parts of Mexico who are "available for service if needed." Among them is Robert Fay, an officer of the German Army and a one-time plotter in New York, who escaped from the Atlanta Penitentiary last August. Fay was serving a sentence for plotting the destruction of munitions ships at sea. One of the men associated with him in that plot, also a German army officer, is also in Mexico, according to the Federal Authorities.

From New York City alone it is estimated that at least 2,000 Germans have gone to Mexico since the dismissal of Count von Bernstorff, and practically all of these men are said to be reserves "available for service if needed." The Germans in Mexico City are said to have formed a military organization, the frame work of which was prepared by Captain von Papen in the last days of the Huerta regime in June 1914.

Known German agents and officials had been known to be working in other parts of Mexico during the Revolution, such as Torreon, Juarez, Chihuahua, and Parral. One of these officials was believed to have instigated one of the Orozco uprisings. The role of these Germans in Mexico would eventually lead to conflicts with American troops across the border.

There were rumors that Villa may have been partially financed by the German imperial government, and some of his military actions were explicitly designed to aid the Kaiser's cause. Felix A. Sommerfeld, described by German historian Friedrich Katz as "one of the most interesting members of the shadowy army of agents, double agents, and lobbyists who swarmed like locusts over Mexico once the revolution had begun," was a con man. Though he'd fought against the revolutionary Boxers in China, he came to Mexico and convinced Madero that he was a revolutionary democrat. Meanwhile he was establishing close relations with the German government and certain US business interests. These interests were represented by a crooked lobbyist named Sherbourne Hopkins, who was closely allied with Carranza. Sherbourne befriended Sommerfeld, gave him money, and told him to go to Mexico to work with Carranza. The silver-tongued Sommerfeld completely won Carranza's trust, and was given the assignment to spy on Villa at Chihuahua. This he did, but not for Carranza; all information on Villa went to the German government. In addition, he ingratiated himself with Villa, who gave him an exclusive concession to import dynamite for his forces. For this, Sommerfeld received a commission of $5,000 a month. In late 1915 (a few months before the attack on Columbus) the US Justice Department ascertained that $340,000 had been paid into Sommerfeld's bank account in St. Louis. The money came from a German government account in New York. When these transactions came to light, Sommerfeld closed the account. Following the money trail, treasury agents learned it had been paid to the Western Cartridge Company, the arms suppliers for Villa. When confronted by agents of the Justice Department, Sommerfeld insisted that he had severed

German intrigues in Mexico escalated throughout the years of the revolution as a means of distracting the United States and preventing the Americans from entering World War I. (AdeQ Historical Archives)

**APRIL 21–
NOVEMBER 23
1914**

**US occupation
of Veracruz**

all relations with Villa after the US recognized Carranza, and sent Villa a telegram protesting the massacre of the 16 mining engineers. Yet he was unable to explain why $340,000 deposited in his account by the German government had ended up in the hands of Villa's arms supplier. Also, according to Carranza's agents in the US, Sommerfeld continued to buy arms for Villa even after his interrogation by the Justice Department. As is often the case, who was using whom?

Pancho Villa was a revolutionary, and the fact that he may have received arms and financial aid from the Germans doesn't mean he embraced Kaiserism. The dominant Carranza–Obregón forces, and the now hostile United States, placed Pancho Villa between a rock and a hard place, so this time he didn't turn down help. Earlier, the German consul in Torreon, which Villa had captured, gave a lavish banquet for him and urged him to march on the Tampico oil fields. With the capture of Tampico, German ships would land in the port and bring him money and arms. Villa appeared to consider the offer, but then changed his mind and marched on Chihuahua. His eventual acceptance of their help was not that Pancho was a German agent, but rather a man engaged in the old game of playing both ends against the middle.

Villa's Anti-Americanism

After years of public and documented support for Villa's fight, the United States, following the diplomatic policies of Woodrow Wilson, who believed that supporting Carranza was the best way to expedite the establishment of a stable Mexican government, refused to allow more arms to be supplied to Villa's army, and allowed Carranza's troops to be relocated over US railroads. Villa felt betrayed by the Americans. He was further enraged by Obregón's use of searchlights, powered by American electricity, to help repel a Villista night attack on the border town of Agua Prieta.

While most sources state that the searchlights that illuminated the battlefield for Calles' machine guns were on the Mexican side of the border, Villa strongly believed that they were on the American side. Additionally, concerned about bullets and artillery shells falling over the border and the possibility of the fighting spilling to the American side, General Frederick Funston stationed three infantry regiments, some cavalry and one regiment of artillery in the cross-border town of Douglas, Arizona. While the American troops in the end did not take part in the fighting, their nearby presence would later lead Villa to believe that the Americans provided Carranza's forces with crucial logistical support, which contributed to his growing anti-Americanism. Villa's belief led him to change his attitude toward the United States. Previously, while engaging in an occasional border raid for supplies, Villa considered himself a friend of the Americans; now he wanted revenge for what he regarded as their treachery.

In January 1916 a group of Villistas attacked a train on the Mexico North Western Railway, near Santa Isabel, Chihuahua, and killed several American employees of ASARCO (American Smelting and Refining Company). The passengers included 18 Americans, 15 of whom worked for ASARCO. There was only one survivor, who gave the details to the press. Villa admitted to ordering the attack, but denied that he had authorized the shedding of American blood.

At Los Tanques on January 18, 1916, Villa and his 200 men, many of whom were comrades from his Dorado elite guard, congregated to discuss upcoming campaigns. Because Villa's army had regained some of its strength and Carranza's stronghold over Mexico appeared to be increasing, Villa informed his men that the moment to attack the Americans had come. However, Villa's initial expedition plans were not geared toward attacking Columbus, New Mexico, but rather the small American town of Presidio across the Rio Grande from Ojinaga in Texas. This is peculiar because Presidio was one of the most destitute and impoverished towns in the United States. The Villistas clearly could not expect to acquire a large quantity of goods or supplies in such a town, but this was true for the majority of the small border towns in Texas. Nonetheless, the anticipated expedition to the Ojinaga region failed due to an unprecedented and highly unexpected degree of desertion. Consequently, Villa's strategies and approach changed drastically in the following weeks.[1]

Protecting the Border

Mounted watchmen of the US Immigration Service patrolled the border in an effort to prevent illegal crossings as early as 1904, but their efforts were irregular and undertaken only when resources permitted. The inspectors, usually called Mounted Guards, operated out of El Paso, Texas. Though they never totaled more than 75, they patrolled as far west as California, trying to restrict the flow of illegal Chinese immigration.

In March 1915 Congress authorized a separate group of Mounted Guards, often referred to as Mounted Inspectors. Most rode on horseback but a few operated cars and even boats. Although these inspectors had broader arrest authority, they still largely pursued Chinese immigrants trying to avoid the Chinese exclusion laws. These patrolmen were Immigrant Inspectors, assigned to inspection stations, and could not watch the border at all times. Military troops along the southwest border performed intermittent border patrolling, but this was secondary to "the more serious work of military training." Illegal aliens encountered in the US by the military were directed to the immigration inspection stations. Texas Rangers were also sporadically assigned to patrol duties by the state, and their efforts were noted as "singularly effective."

Throughout 1915 Mexican insurgents raided the Texas border region as part of the Plan de San Diego. Supported by the Mexican Carranza government, a group of raiders known as the Seditionists attacked American military and commercial interests along the US–Mexican border in an effort to provoke a race war in the Southwestern United States with aims of returning the area to Mexican control. Charged with guarding the border, American General Frederick Funston had 20,000 troops to pit against the few hundred Seditionist insurgents. Nonetheless, the Mexicans never raided in force and the long border was difficult for Funston to fully protect. The

---

1 Frederick Katz, *The Life and Times of Pancho Villa*, p.560

A cavalryman displaying his kit prior to riding out on patrol somewhere along the US–Mexican Border. Barely visible is the scabbard tip for the Model 1913 Cavalry Saber. The saber was designed by 2nd Lieutenant (later General) George S. Patton in 1913, when he was Master of the Sword at the Mounted Service School, and is commonly referred to as the Patton Saber. (AdeQ Historical Archives)

Seditionist raids became such a threat to the Americans in the Big Bend area that local vigilante groups were formed in order to repel the Mexican raiders, as Funston did not have enough troops to ensure the safety of the American citizens living in the area.

In order to protect the Big Bend region, the United States deployed a number of US Cavalry and Signal Corps personnel in various posts along the Texas border. One of these posts was at the village of Ojo de Agua, which had been raided on September 3, 1915 and was the planned target of a Seditionist raid in October 1916. The American base at Ojo de Agua under the command of Sergeant Ernest Schaeffer consisted of a radio station manned by approximately ten men from Troop G, 3rd Cavalry and eight men of the United States Army Signal Corps. The post at Ojo de Agua was lightly defended and seemed to be little match for the 25–100 raiders that planned to raid the village.

After crossing the Rio Grande and arriving at Ojo de Agua at approximately 1a.m., the Mexican raiders attacked the village's garrison. The American soldiers who had been sleeping in a wooden building stubbornly resisted. The Americans were heavily outgunned though, as the Signal Corps personnel were armed only with pistols. In the fighting Sergeant Schaeffer was killed, and as a result command devolved to Sergeant First Class Herbert Reeves Smith who by that time had also been wounded three times. In addition to attacking the garrison, the raiders robbed the post office and attacked the home of the Dillard family, setting their house on fire and stealing their livestock.

Although the Americans at Ojo de Agua were unable to call for reinforcements due to the fact that their wireless station had been knocked out of action earlier in the attack, other American detachments in the vicinity heard gunfire and two groups of American cavalry set out to investigate. A company from the 3rd Cavalry under Captain Frank Ross McCoy at

Mission, Texas, some 8 miles from Ojo de Agua was dispatched, as was a small group of 12 recruits under Captain W. J. Scott. As Scott's outfit was only 2 miles from the fighting, they arrived at the scene well before McCoy did and immediately attacked from the west of the raiders' positions, driving them off from their assault on the mission. McCoy's force arrived just as the Mexicans withdrew and saw little or no fighting.

By the end of the raid one civilian and three American soldiers had been killed, including the Ojo de Agua post's commanding officer, Sergeant Schaffer, and eight wounded. The Seditionists also took several casualties, with five men dead and at least nine others wounded, of whom two later died. A Japanese man was found among the dead, as were two Carranzistas soldiers, a fact which was seen as evidence that the Carranzistas had been supporting the Plan de San Diego. The American soldiers were commended for their bravery during the raid, and Sergeant First Class Reeves was awarded a Distinguished Service Cross for his actions during the engagement.

The Seditionist raid on Ojo de Agua had a vast impact on American military strategy in the area. The severity of the raid led the commanding American general in the region, General Frederick Funston, to reinforce the Texas–Mexico border region with troops and to contact Washington with demands that he be allowed to give no quarter to any Mexican raiders who attacked the United States in the future. Although Washington denied General Funston his request, the raids did come to an end when Washington finally gave diplomatic recognition to the Mexican government under Carranza. Wishing to maintain good relations with the American government, Carranza ordered the Seditionist commanders to cease their raiding activities. Without support from the Mexican federal government the Plan de San Diego movement fell apart and there were no further Mexican invasions of the United States until the Villista raids began in 1916.

THE RAID ON COLUMBUS

A series of meetings were held between an Associated Press correspondent, Mr. George L. Seese, and a Villista agent. The agent wanted to convey to the Americans via their press that Villa had nothing to do with the massacre of Americans at Santa Ysabel and wanted to punish his subordinate, Pablo Lopez, who committed the atrocity. This alleged agent of Villa agreed to take a letter to Villa suggesting the wisdom of going to Washington and seeing President Wilson. About a week later Seese received a verbal reply, ostensibly from Villa, that he considered the plan feasible and that he would be glad to accompany the Associated Press correspondent to Washington, provided he could be assured of a safe conduct. On March 2, 1916, one week previous to the Columbus Raid, the Associated Press forbade their agent to continue with the scheme, and Villa was so notified. Many believe that Villa possibly fostered this scheme as a blind to his real intentions, as his private papers, found on the Columbus battlefield, proved that he had planned as early as January 6 to make an attack upon Columbus.

On March 8, 1916 the *El Paso Times* reported:

VILLA EXPECTED TO ATTACK PALOMAS

Information received in El Paso last night from the 13th Cavalry, stationed at Columbus, New Mexico, was to the effect that Villa had been sighted 15 miles west of Palomas Monday night and was camped there all day Tuesday. What his plans are at this time are not known.

Villa is reported to have between 300 to 400 men with him. They are all well mounted and since arriving near Palomas have been slaughtering large numbers of cattle.

There is but a small Carranza garrison at Palomas and it is believed that Villa intends making an attack on the town.

Palomas rested just across the border from Columbus, New Mexico. This small frontier town had a population of about 300 and consisted of a cluster of adobe houses and wooden buildings. The basic layout of the sunbaked dirt streets of Columbus consisted of Broadway, the main street, which ran east and west; it boasted a hardware store operated by J. L. Walker; J. T. Dean's grocery; C. Dewitt Miller's drug store; the Hoover Hotel; and a score of smaller businesses.

The most pretentious of the businesses there was that of the Ravel Brothers Mercantile, located on Boulevard Street. Louis and Sam Ravel handled hardware goods, cooking utensils, boots, overalls, and all of the sundry articles for the residents living in the area. The brothers lived in the rear of the store with their younger sibling, 12-year-old Arthur. They enjoyed the patronage of Mexicans from across the border and encouraged trade with the Mexicans that included guns and ammunition. It is believed that the brothers sold huge quantities of munitions to the Villistas. Local lore states that the brothers short-changed Villa by not delivering the $2,500-worth of goods that the Mexican "General" had paid for, thereby giving reason for the raid.

On Taft Street, near the railroad station, was the two-story frame Commercial Hotel, operated by Mr. and Mrs. W. T. Ritchie. Across from that was a movie theater. Opposite the railroad tracks, south of town, was the army encampment where soldiers of the 13th United States Cavalry Regiment (four troops of the regiment and a machine-gun platoon), under the command of Colonel Herbert J. Slocum, were quartered. The soldiers arrived there and established it as the regimental headquarters since September 1912. The encampment was known as Camp Furlong.

A modern-day view of the town of Columbus, New Mexico, as seen from Villa Hill (formerly Coote's Hill) and the vantage point from which the Villistas attacked. In the foreground and to the right of the photo is the site of Camp Furlong. In the center are the customs house and the railroad depot. Beyond is the small town of Columbus. (Author's photo)

The headquarters building, the shack for the officer of the day, a shack occupied by the surgeon, and the quartermaster's storehouse were on the west edge of the camp on the Guzman-Deming Road; the guard house and stables were located on the east edge of camp, and the barracks and mess shacks lay in between. In addition to the Guzman-Deming Road another road meandered through the eastern part of camp. These roads were open to traffic night and day.

The barracks were flimsy wooden structures, the stables were open sheds, but the mess shacks and hospital were bulletproof, made of adobe (mud) bricks. Across the Guzman-Deming Road and the El Paso and Southwestern railroad track opposite the Columbus Railroad Depot was the customs station where US customs agents would stop anyone approaching south of the tracks. Directly in front of the customs station was a huge arroyo – a natural ditch that ran parallel to the road the full 3 miles to the border. Behind the customs house is a small hill of dark lava stone and scant brush known as Coote's Hill or sometimes referred to as Villa Hill since the raid. Between this hill and the ditch was an adobe house occupied by two officers. The other officers of the regiment were quartered throughout the village but not more than three or four hundred yards distant from camp. Three miles south of Columbus is the US/Mexican boundary line. Exactly 32 miles north from Columbus, straddling Highway 80, is the prosperous town of Deming.

A high wire fence marks the border, running east and west for several miles. A Mexican customs station was located in Palomas, a treeless, sunbaked quaint village of squat adobe buildings, surrounded by the limitless brush. A small garrison of Carranzistas soldiers provided scant protection for the border town.

On the afternoon of March 8, 1916, Juan Favela, an employee of the extensive Palomas Land & Cattle Company, was riding through the high mesquite 5 miles south of the border with some *vaqueros* rounding up stray cattle. The Palomas Land & Cattle Company was an American-owned enterprise that owned a lot of land on the Mexican side of the border.

Favela left his men and headed toward the ranch located several miles to the west; as he topped a hill he spied a large Villista force heading for the border. He immediately turned his steed about and raced toward Columbus, warning the Carranzista soldiers as he raced through the Mexican customs station and headed for the American military encampment 3 miles north. There, he demanded an audience with Colonel Slocum. Favela reported that he'd seen a force of approximately 500 Villistas and that "they were heading for the border; they were just south of Palomas; they would raid Columbus before dawn!"[2] Colonel Slocum calmly told Favela to go get a drink and dismissed the warning as hysteria. Slocum's attitude could be explained by the fact that the reports coming in were so ambiguous and contradictory that it was nearly impossible for Slocum to construct an accurate depiction of the circumstances.

---

2 Harris, *Pancho Villa and the Columbus* Raid, p.87

In the months prior to the raid on Columbus, prospects of Villa initiating a border attack had long been considered by American government and military officials. In fact, raids on US soil from across the border had occurred with alarming frequency. From July 1915 to June 1916 there were 38 raids on the US by Mexican bandits, which resulted in the death of 37 US citizens, 26 of them soldiers. Evidence that Villa and his men were making their way toward the New Mexico border was made known to US officials in as early as February of 1916, but they were unable to successfully track his movements due to a lack of financial resources that prevented them from hiring secret service agents. As a result, the only means they had to acquire information in regard to Villa's location was based solely on information the Carranzistas offered, but the majority of such accounts were questionable.

Colonel Slocum, commander of the small garrison encamped in Columbus at the time of the Villista Raid. (Pancho Villa State Park)

The information that appeared both genuine and credible was telegraphed on March 3 to the State Department by Zach Cobb, the US collector of customs at El Paso, Texas. Cobb delivered this information after he allegedly witnessed Villa and approximately 300 men near Madero, Chihuahua, heading north toward Columbus, New Mexico. In the telegraph Cobb stated that there was "reason to believe" Villa intended "to cross to the United States" and "to proceed to Washington." Villa was previously reported to be near the Casas Grandes River, 45 miles southwest of Columbus, and at the Rancho Nogales, approximately 65 miles southwest of Columbus. Although this newly acquired information was believed to be reliable, its credibility was short-lived.

Three days later, on March 6, journalists were notified by the Carranzista General Gavira in Juarez that, contrary to popular belief, Villa had no intention of reporting to Washington. Instead, Gavira stated to George L. Seese, a US correspondent to Villa, that Villa "intended to cause some incident that would force the United States to intervene in Mexico."[3] This information was conveyed to General John J. Pershing of the United States Army, who questioned its credibility due to the contradictory nature of all the reports regarding Villa's whereabouts. Pershing understood it was unrealistic to establish the truth by any means other than concrete reconnaissance, which was unthinkable. Furthermore, Pershing had acquired disconcerting

---

3 Tompkins, p.42

information at his post at Fort Bliss from his own intelligent sources dating back to September of 1915 regarding a possible attack on the United States by Villa. His sources stated that Villa would attack El Paso, Texas, with a force of 15,000 men if the United States recognized Carranza as de facto President. This inevitably led the general to view El Paso as Villa's most likely target. All of these reports were additionally sent to Colonel Herbert J. Slocum.

To his dismay, Colonel Slocum was unable to verify any information on Villa's whereabouts or intentions. He arranged further patrols and strengthened his positions, but this was the extent of his capacity to safeguard his territory. The colonel was accountable for 65 miles of uninhabited border that stretched from Hermanas in the west to Noria in the east. Furthermore, the number of troops under his authority was exceptionally small to encompass such a vast region. His regiment consisted of 21 officers and 530 soldiers, 79 of which were non-combatants. Altogether, Slocum possessed approximately one officer for every 600 feet of border. Slocum had dispatched two officers and 65 men at Palomas at an outpost to the east, and Major Lindsey controlled seven officers and 151 men 11 miles at another to the west – thereby leaving roughly 120 soldiers in Columbus.

As the day ended many of the regimental senior officers retired to their rental homes located outside of the camp and within the town of Columbus. Slocum and several other officers boarded the train to attend a dance in Deming that night, not to return until morning. Lieutenant Castleman took charge of Camp Furlong as Officer of the Day and inspected the border patrol after the coming down of the flag at retreat.

For a number of days prior to March 9 locals of the tiny town began noticing scenes that weren't everyday occurrences. Dr. Roy Edward Stivison, a local school principal, recounted: "We had noticed and commented on the large number of strange Mexicans appearing in and about the town. We found out later these were spies from the Villista forces ranging just south

Coote's Hill (Villa Hill) covered the Villista approach toward Columbus and was where Villa ordered the attack. After the raid the hill was incorporated as a part of the growing Camp Furlong and used as an observation post by the army. (Photo by the author)

of the border."[4] The day prior to the attack, Pancho Villa ordered a final reconnaissance of the town of Columbus and was advised by Colonel Cipriano Vargas that there were only about 30 American soldiers at the encampment. This was later to prove a miscalculation as the garrison was four times greater than the Villistas had observed. The revolutionary leader Francisco "Pancho" Villa, (Colonel) Francisco Beltrán, (Colonel) Candelario Cervantes, (General) Nicolás Fernández, and (General) Pablo Lopez held a council of war to decide upon a plan of action. Villa's plan of attack was to split his force into two columns and adhered to a specific strategy by approaching the garrison and town from opposite positions from both the east and west. One column was to strike the commercial district where the raiders would loot the stores for clothing and blankets as well as other supplies. The second column was to execute a surprise attack upon Camp Furlong by targeting the horse stables, weapons' room, and the food supplies.

At 4p.m. the column moved north and sometime after midnight crossed the border through a hole cut in the fence a mile west of Palomas. As they moved eastward toward the big ditch, "A signal passed down the line of riders for a halt. As they waited, three men merged out of the darkness. They held a brief consultation with Villa... These three Villistas, experts with knives, crawled up to an American army outpost and killed the two soldiers on duty there. Captain 'Bull' Studgy's outpost, a quarter mile farther east, was by-passed."[5]

Deploying his men around the sleeping desert town, their presence was virtually undetectable as they followed the hidden trench (arroyo) that progressed directly through the center of the garrison and town, helped by a lack of adequate lighting; Columbus' only source of light emitted from

The U.S. Customs House, built in 1902, regulated trade coming across the border from Palomas, Mexico, several miles to the south. In 1901, it was a sub-port of the customs house in El Paso, Texas. The building, an example of Prairie School architecture, stood along the arroyo from where the Villistas hid and from where they made their attack upon Columbus. The building is now part of the Pancho Villa State Park. (Photo by the Author)

MARCH 9 1916

Raid on Columbus, New Mexico

4 Stivison, p.37
5 Larry A. Harris, p.87

The railroad depot was in the middle of the crossfire between Villista and American troops as evidenced by the clock that was stopped by a bullet in the early morning of the attack. (Pancho Villa State Park)

kerosene lamps placed sporadically throughout the town. "Every man was armed with a rifle, pistol and bandoleer. Tied to many of the saddles were five gallon cans of kerosene."[6] Around four in the morning of March 9, 1916 Villa raised his arm and the battle cry of "*Vayanse adelante, muchachos!*" was sounded. The attack began with cries of "*Viva Villa*," "*Viva Mexico*," and "*Muerto a los Gringos!*" This was confirmed by a clock outside the railroad station that was struck by a stray bullet, causing it to stop at 4:11a.m. shortly after the first shots rang out.

Immediately three groups of Villistas began swarming Columbus and Camp Furlong from various directions. One of these had entered the camp by way of a dry arroyo; another had entered the town and was ready to begin looting the stores as soon as it was safe to do so. As the Villistas advanced into the town, they drenched each business building as they came to it and put it to the torch. Soon the entire area was illuminated by dancing flames. The remaining unit passed into the corrals and was scattering horses before any firing took place.

Upon hearing the first shots at about 4:15a.m., the Officer of the Day, Lieut. James P. Castleman, ran to the guard tent, shooting a Villista on the way, and turned out the guard. He then joined up with his F Troop, 13th Cavalry, which had been formed by Sergeant Michael Fody. The camp and town were under

---

6 Boucher, p.12

American National Guardsmen training with a Hotchkiss M1909 Benet-Mercie machine gun in .30-06 caliber. US forces used the Benet-Mercie in the Pancho Villa Expedition in Mexico of 1916–17 and initially in France. Firing pins and extractors broke frequently on the American guns; United States troops called the M1909 the "daylight gun" because of the difficulty replacing broken parts at night, and the unfortunate jams created when the loading strips were accidentally inserted upside down in darkness.
(AdeQ Historical Archives)

a general attack from two directions. Minutes later Lieut. John P. Lucas, who had just returned on the midnight train from El Paso, where he had been participating in regimental polo matches, saw a horseman ride by his window. He was wearing a high-peaked sombrero characteristic of the Villistas. Hurrying outside, he joined the attackers, who were running toward the barracks, the darkness concealing his identity. Reaching the barracks of his machine gun troop, he led his men to the guard tent where their weapons were under lock and key. Despite several incidents of the French-made Benet-Mercier machine guns jamming, the four gun crews managed to loose 20,000 rounds at the enemy. The Benet-Mercier did not use belts of ammunition but instead depended upon timely insertion of long stripper clips. Operating the gun in the early morning darkness required an expert crew to prevent jamming – something not present in Columbus, New Mexico, in 1916.

After fighting in camp for 30 or 40 minutes, the soldiers began to gain the upper hand and then were able to send aid to the beleaguered citizens. Lieutenant Castleman ordered the troop on toward the town, where the heaviest firing was concentrated. They threw a cordon of troops across the main street and thus kept the bandits from entering the north part of town. Sergeant Fody recounted the following:

PREVIOUS PAGES

The attack on Columbus, New Mexico, by Villistas. It was at the intersection of Broadway and East Boundary Streets where Lieutenant Castleman chose to set up his line of defense with their Benet-Mercie machine guns firing down Broadway Street. This kept the Villistas from robbing the bank or up East Boundary Street where Colonel Slocum lived, as did Lieutenant Castleman's wife. The covering firing by the Americans helped some of the townspeople seek refuge in the Hoover Hotel. Others weren't so lucky: Mrs. Milton James, who was pregnant, attempted to run to the hotel for protection but was shot down by the Villistas, along with her husband. A resident of the hotel was also killed as he attempted to run to his business to secure some weapons.

... at the command "Forward March," every man jumped to his feet without a scratch and advanced. After crossing the railroad track we had our first man hit, Private Jesse P. Taylor, who was shot in the leg. I told him to lie down and be quiet and that we would pick him up on our return. Advancing about ten yards farther Private Ravielle tripped over barbed wire, discharging his piece in front of his nose, the concussion of which made his nose bleed. We made about four stands in about five hundred yards. Private Thomas Butler was hit during the second stand but would not give up and went on with us until he was hit five distinct times, the last one proving fatal.

We advanced and took position on the Main Street near the town bank, having a clear field of fire. For over an hour we lay in this position but were unable to do effective work on account of the darkness. As soon as it began to light up our ammunition was getting low. I sent Private Dobrowalski to the guard house after some ammunition, he had to get three Mexicans who disputed his way before he could comply with his orders.

When the Mexicans set fire to the Commercial Hotel, the blaze illuminated the section. We were then in the dark and had the advantage. The group of which I was a member, numbering twenty-five men under Lieutenant Castleman, was the largest group under one command during the fight. Our forces were scattered in little bunches throughout the camp and vicinity but did very telling work. As soon as the light was bright enough we made every shot count and soon thoroughly discouraged the invaders. About 6:30 the Mexican bugler sounded "Recall," it was a welcome sound. The Mexicans began immediately to retreat. Major Frank Tompkins obtained permission from Colonel Slocum to give pursuit.[7]

There had been various accounts of the strike from the residents and soldiers. Once the attack commenced, the Mexicans' first act was to stampede the cavalry horses. The remaining unit of the two columns formed from Villa's forces were to pass into the corrals and scatter the horses before any firing took place. However, as the Mexicans were in the process of stampeding the horses their moment of surprise was taken away when they were happened upon by an American trooper. An army sergeant who had claimed credit for firing the first shot and for killing the first Villista described the following to Dr. R. E. Stivison: "I happened to be awake about four o'clock and while coming around one side of one of the barracks found myself face to face with a Mexican who was pointing his gun at me. I pulled my army pistol and shot him in his tracks."[8] Apparently, according to the sergeant this was the signal for general firing to commence.

One account has it that the Villistas were searching for a merchant who cheated Pancho Villa. It was claimed that the Villistas were shouting Sam Ravel's name not knowing that he had left for a dental appointment in El Paso. Sam's brother and partner, Louis, wasn't so lucky. He was in the store the brothers owned when the Villistas struck. He burrowed his way under a huge pile of cowhides and prayed. His prayers must have been been answered, because the bandits overturned the place looking for Sam, at the

---

7 Tompkins, p.80
8 Stivison, p.42

same time looting the store of everything of value, and destroying the rest. The pile of cowhides didn't escape their notice either. They tore the heap apart, but stopped before reaching the bottom, and it is well that they did, for underneath the last lay the shivering Louis.

Arthur, the 12-year-old brother of the Ravels, ran out of the building and raced up the street in his underwear. He tried his best to escape but was captured after a short chase by two Villistas. They were caught in a crossfire where the Villistas were killed by American gunfire and the young Ravel ran as fast as he could toward the outskirts of Columbus.

Dr. Stivison stated that "About five o'clock flames began to appear from the big frame Ritchie Hotel and from the Lemmon Store just across the street from it. In the lurid light we could distinguish men dashing hither and thither and riderless horses running about in all directions. The continuous firing, the shouting of the Mexicans, and confusion in general continued until about seven o'clock. Then with the coming of daylight, the firing diminished and finally ceased altogether."[9]

As the first streaks of sunlight began appearing, Villa realized that without darkness he and his men could not hope to survive, and so ordered his bugler to sound the retreat. The retreat was orderly and well planned but Villa did not plan on losing so many of his men. At full gallop and with a fine assortment of booty including over 100 horses and mules and 300 rifles, the Mexicans galloped for the canyon-slashed sierras to the south. Well over 60 Villistas were scattered about in the streets of Columbus.

As daylight came and the sounds of gunfire ceased, a few of the townspeople began venturing out to the streets. Dr. Stivison recounted:

We ventured out of our house and started toward Reverend Boddington's block. We met the good man and his wife coming out, as bewildered as we were, Together we set out for the main part of town. Coming to the Walker Hardware Store we found our old friend and neighbor, James Dean, a grocery merchant, lying in the middle of the street, his body riddled with bullets. We learned that he had thought the Lemmon Store had been set afire accidentally and that he might be of assistance in putting it out. The raiders got him before he reached the scene of the blaze.

Continuing to the Ritchie Hotel, we found the body of Mr. Ritchie with his legs partly burned off, lying beside the building. His wife told us later that he had offered the Villistas all the money in his pocket ($50.00) if they would spare his life. They took the money but shot him and threw his body into the burning hotel. Rings were taken forcibly from Mrs. Ritchie's hands. Their little daughter, Edna, a pupil of mine, showed me holes in the back of her coat, put there by the bandits as she was escaping down the back stairs.

Five men, guests of the hotel, were taken with Mr. Ritchie and all met the same tragic fate. One of these was a Mr. Walker, who with his wife had come the day before to attend the Sunday School convention. He was yanked from his wife's arms and shot. Young Señor Perera, a representative of the Mexican consulate at El Paso, was another

---

9 Stivison, p.41

The Villistas broke into the Columbus State Bank on Broadway Street and tried to smash their way into the vault without success. The vault's steel door and frame are preserved in the Columbus Historical Museum (former railroad depot) where traces of numerous dents from Villista bullets can be seen. Remains of the concrete vault marks the site where the bank, which was turned into a temporary morgue, once stood. (Author's photo)

of the guests who met an untimely end. He had volunteered to take the place of the regular representative, Mr. Gray, who was ill at the time. Perera was indeed a prize for the Villistas. His body was found the next morning just across the line.[10]

Dr. Stivison continued on to the camp hospital and found a pump foreman for the El Paso and Southwestern Rail Road severely wounded. His house was situated on the south side of the tracks in the very center of the fighting. His wife, Bessie James, was lying dead at the Hoover Hotel. She and her husband had been shot at the hotel's entrance as they sought refuge from the fighting in the streets. As Stivison continued surveying the carnage in and around Columbus, he remembered the following:

> We found the body of our good friend, C.C. Miller, the druggist, lying in the door of his store. He had left the Hoover Hotel and started for the drug store but was mortally wounded just as he reached its sheltering walls. Mr. Miller had been a particularly fine character. He had come to the Mimbres Valley as a tubercular, obtained a herd of goats and lived in the open until he had regained his health, then resumed his vocation of druggist.

> In the Hoover Hotel, seriously wounded, we found Mrs. J. J. Moore, wife of one of the merchants. The Moores had a beautiful little home between Columbus and the border. The bandits, in their retreat, had stopped there long enough to bring death and destruction to it. Mr. Moore had been shot and instantly killed before his wife's eyes. Mrs. Moore had run from the house and was climbing through a wire fence

---

10 Stivison, p.41

On March 9, 1916 when Pancho Villa attacked from Mexico this hotel was the center of some of the heaviest fighting. William Christopher Hoover owned the hotel and was the Mayor of Columbus at the time of the raid. (AdeQ Historical Archives/author)

when she was shot through the right thigh. ... Dead Villistas were lying in the streets all over town. Many were mere boys, fourteen to sixteen years old. Many of the dead and dying had taken crucifixes from their pockets and were clutching them against their breasts.[11]

American casualties amounted to 18 killed; eight were soldiers and ten were civilians, one of whom was a woman. However, the Villista's casualties far exceeded those of the Americans'. In addition, unbeknownst to Juan Favela, who reported to Colonel Slocum prior to the raid, Villistas had captured three Americans from the Palomas Land & Cattle Company. Two of the captives were hanged and the third man was shot when efforts to horse-trample him failed.

Colonel Slocum authorized Major Frank Tompkins of the 13th US Cavalry to mount up a troop and pursue the fleeing Villistas. Tompkins quickly rounded up Captain Rudolph Smyser's Troop H and with 32 men left camp. The troop proceeded southwest and in the dim light of the morning saw the Mexican column retreating toward the border. The troopers

---

11 Stivison, p.42

THE VILLISTA RAID ON COLUMBUS, NEW MEXICO

MARCH 9, 1916

The raid on Columbus was a multi-pronged attack upon the military camp of the 13th US Cavalry and the town itself by Pancho Villa's men from their hidden positions behind Coote's Hill and in the arroyo (ditch) that ran parallel to the road leading toward the Mexican border.

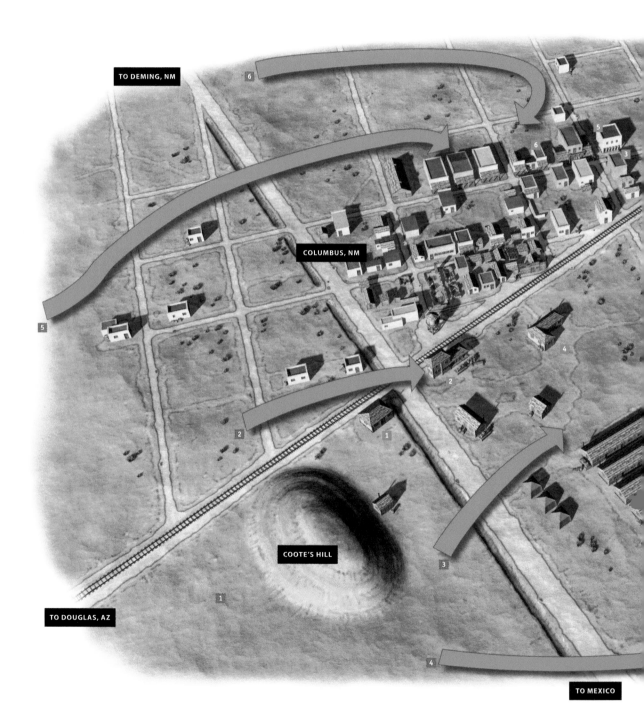

TO DEMING, NM

COLUMBUS, NM

COOTE'S HILL

TO DOUGLAS, AZ

TO MEXICO

VILLISTA FORCES [1]-[6]

1. Villa (40 men)
2. Lopez (100 men)
3. Cervantes (120 men)
4. Pedrosa (40 men)
5. Fernandez (60 men)
6. Beltran (125 men)

LOCATIONS IN COLUMBUS, NM [1]-[6]

1. Custom House
2. Railroad Depot
3. Hoover Hotel
4. Hospital
5. Bank
6. Newspaper Office

TO EL PASO, TX

CAMP FURLONG

As daylight came to Columbus the evidence of the carnage became clearer. Destroyed in the fire were a block of buildings consisting of the Commercial Hotel, Lemmon & Romney Mercantile, and two small houses. It was here that the greatest number of American deaths occurred. (AdeQ Historical Archives)

paralleled their march with the objective of cutting off as many as possible as soon as they could get clear of the wire fences at the border.

An isolated hill stood about 300 yards south of the fence between the Mexican column and Tompkins' forces. The hill was occupied by Villistas who were a covering detachment for their left flank. The troopers cut the fence to the east of the hill deployed as foragers and advanced, increasing the pace until the command of "Charge!" was cried out. As the troopers charged the slopes of the hill the Villistas broke and ran. Tompkins recounted, "We galloped to the hill top, returned pistols, dismounted, and opened rifle fire on the fleeing Mexicans killing thirty-two men and many horses."[12]

Realizing that they were now in Mexican territory against a standing War Department order, Tompkins sent a note to Colonel Slocum stating that the Mexicans had taken up positions on a ridge 1500 yards to the south of the international boundary between the United States and Mexico, and requested permission to take Troop G with his men of Troop H to continue the pursuit. Approximately 45 minutes later Slocum responded that Tompkins could use his own judgment. While Troop G was diverted by firing heard at the border gate, Tompkins was joined by men of Troop F and continued the pursuit. Within 45 minutes he struck Villa's rear guard.

Major Tompkins described the following: "We deployed at wide intervals and advanced toward the enemy at a fast trot, the enemy firing all the time but their shots going wild. When we were within four hundred yards of them, finding good shelter for the horses, we dismounted, and opened fire, driving the rear guard back on the main body and killing and wounding quite a few. It may be well to state here that the men dismounted while extended, each man linking his horse to his stirrup buckle thus keeping the animal immobile

---

12 Tompkins, p.57

Disposing of Bodies on a Mexican Battlefield.

and allowing every rifle to get on the firing line and get there fast. For this kind of fighting where the horses were in a fold of the ground but a few yards behind their riders, this method of linking enabled the men to dismount and mount with speed."[13]

Tompkins again took up the pursuit and overtook the rear guard within 30 minutes. They tried to turn the Villistas on their left flank but exposed the troopers to fire at close range. Tompkins was slightly injured in the knee and a Captain Williams was wounded in the hand. The troopers dismounted under cover and advanced to within view of the enemy while Troop F was firing at the main body at 800 yards and Troop H firing at the Mexican rear guard with battle sights. They eventually drove back the Villistas and took up the pursuit once again. The troopers counted an additional twelve dead Mexicans. Thinking that the Villistas were going to take up a position on an elevation, Tompkins detached Troop F to flank this position while he proceeded on the Mexican trail with Troop H. Tompkins wrote: "I again overtook the enemy, but this time on a plain devoid of cover. They soon saw our weakness (but twenty-nine men) and started an attack with at least three hundred men while the remainder of the Mexican forces continued their retreat. We returned their fire until one horse was wounded and one killed when we fell back about four hundred yards where our horses had excellent cover. But the Mexicans refused to advance against us in this new position."[14]

An inglorious death: after the raid the bodies of the Villistas were gathered outside the town, piled like firewood, doused with gasoline, and burned. The stench of decaying human and horse flesh out in the desert continued on in the following months. (AdeQ Historical Archives)

---

13 Tompkins, p.56
14 Tompkins, p.56

Archibald Douglass Frost, his wife Mary Alice, and their 6-month-old son fled Columbus in this 1915 Dodge Touring Car during the Pancho Villa raid. Mr. Frost was shot twice and the vehicle sprayed with gunfire as they sped through Columbus toward Deming. Mary Alice, an inexperienced driver, had to take the wheel on several occasions. The three arrived in Deming, and upon examining the Dodge found numerous bullet holes, including two through the driver's seat. Frost carried one of the bullets in his body for the rest of his life; it is currently preserved in the museum of the Pancho Villa State Park. (Author's photo)

With ammunition running low and the men as well as their horses exhausted from fighting without food or water, Major Tompkins returned to Columbus. The American counter-attack took the troopers within 15 miles of Mexican territory. As a result of the pursuit, many of Tompkins' officers and men "counted between seventy-five and one hundred dead Villistas on Mexican soil as well as many wounded or killed horses and mules, the abandonment of two machine guns by the Mexicans, many rifles and pistols, much ammunition, food stuff and loot which had been taken at Columbus."[15] In addition to the Americans' quick response during the Villista surprise attack upon Columbus and Camp Furlong, after seven and one half hours of hard riding, covering approximately 30 miles of rough country, fighting four separate rear-guard actions without the loss of a single American soldier, and inflicting heavy losses on the retreating Villistas, Tompkins and his fellow officers managed to turn Pancho Villa's raid into a fiasco, the repercussions of which were to follow Villa and his men in the months to come.

The days following the raid soldiers from Fort Bliss were pouring into Columbus making it the safest town on the border. Several townspeople, fearing further attacks, were permitted to stay in the clubroom of Troop F in Camp Furlong, with the soldiers providing pillows and bedding. Within the next few days after the attack the bodies of the soldiers were sent east for burial. President Carranza's personal representative, General Garcia, was present with his staff at a little ceremony at the station in which soldiers and regimental bands took part. Dr. Stivison recounted: "During the morning of the same day, we saw military wagons gathering up the bodies of the bandits. These were taken to the edge of town, placed in a pile,

**MARCH 15
1916**

**The Punitive
Expedition
crosses into
Mexico**

---

15 Tompkins, p.56

Most of the civilians killed in the raid were buried in the Valley Heights Cemetery, including: Henry Arthur McKinney, Bessie James, James T. Dean, and Perrow G. Moseley. Those soldiers killed in the raid were taken back to Fort Bliss by rail and were interned at the National Cemetery there. (Author's photo)

saturated with kerosene, and burned. It was a grisly sight but we were glad to know that these particular men would no longer be a menace to the peace of the border."[16]

Mexican losses during and immediately after the raid were believed to be considerable. While returning to Columbus following the pursuit of the Villistas, a distance of approximately 15 miles, nearly 100 dead Villistas were counted by the Americans. Supplementary to the bodies counted on the journey home, 67 Villista corpses were discovered in Columbus the morning after the raid. These were placed in a large heap just beyond the edge of town (approximately 1 mile east), soaked with gasoline, and cremated. For more than a day the fires seethed before ultimately going out while even longer the acrid odor of smoldering flesh saturated the air. One source claimed that "it was estimated that between 175 and 200 bodies were in that grisly pile, not including the dead horses."[17] These numbers reveal the consequences the Villistas suffered for their actions in Columbus.

MARCH 29 1916

7th Cavalry attacks Guerrero

---

16 Stivison, p.43
17 Harris, *Pancho Villa and the Columbus Raid*, p.92

THE PUNITIVE EXPEDITION

In the days following the raid, Americans across United States read sensational headlines.

- Villa invades the US
- Bandits burn and kill in Columbus
- American torn from wife's arms, shot like a dog and roasted
- Mexican thug who has defied United States and American victims
- Death to Americans! Pancho's cry; wants to choke hated gringo
- Snipers fire at victims fleeing to find shelter from fusilade
- Four American ranchers said to be hanged south of the border
- Carranza to get a real firm note on outrage

The American public demanded revenge for the Columbus Raid, and public opinion at the time clamored for action to be taken by the United States. (AdeQ Historical Archives)

In no time Americans and the press demanded revenge for the outrage committed by General Villa and his men in Columbus. The Wilson administration also began implementing a plan on how to punish Villa.

To lead the expedition, US Army Chief of Staff Major General Hugh Scott selected Brigadier General John J. Pershing. A veteran of the Indian Wars and Philippine Insurrection, Pershing was also known for his diplomatic skills and tact. Attached to Pershing's staff was a young lieutenant who would later become famous, George S. Patton. While Pershing worked to marshal his forces, Secretary of State Robert Lansing lobbied Carranza into allowing American troops to cross the border.

While motions were being made for an army to be prepared for an expedition, Secretary of State Robert Lansing negotiated with Venustiano Carranza to allow the United States to enter Mexico without interference. Carranza balked at granting approval for the expedition. As a compromise, he insisted that his own

troops would track down Villa. The United States refused his offer, and after a week of fervent bartering Carranza reluctantly agreed to allow the Americans across the border as long as they strayed no further than the state of Chihuahua. The army was under the impression that Carranza would allow the expedition to ship supplies over the Mexican Northwestern Railway, but initially he refused. Several weeks into the expedition, Carranza made some concessions and allowed the Americans to use the railroad, but by then supplies were already moving by horse and primitive Dodge trucks. The army's telegraph lines also needed constant attention since the Mexicans made a sport of cutting the wires. The Punitive Expedition learned the hard way that Carranza had little interest in cooperating with the efforts to capture Villa.

Major General Hugh Lenox Scott wrote in his memoirs:

Venustiano Carranza de la Garza was one of the leaders of the Mexican Revolution. He ultimately became President of Mexico following the overthrow of the dictatorial Huerta regime in the summer of 1914 and during his administration the current constitution of Mexico was drafted. (AdeQ Historical Archives)

> Secretary of War Newton D. Baker, new on the job, called Chief of Staff of the Army, Major General Hugh L. Scott, into a huddle and told him, "I want to start an expedition into Mexico to catch Villa."
>
> This seemed strange ... and I asked: "Mr. Secretary, do you want the United States to make war on one man? Suppose he should get onto a train and go to Guatemala, Yucatan, or South America; are you going to go after him?"
>
> He said, "Well, no, I am not."
>
> "That is not what you want then. You want his band captured or destroyed," I suggested.
>
> "Yes," he said, "that is what I really want."
>
> And after his approval the ... telegram was sent to General Funston ... in which it will be seen that no mention is made of the capture of Villa himself.

Funston received that telegram on March 10. It gave him the go-ahead to organize the Punitive Expedition and named Brigadier General John J. Pershing as commander. The objective was to subdue the Mexican revolutionary forces and to capture Francisco (Pancho) Villa. This turned out to be an exceedingly difficult military task, especially in view of the fact that General Pershing's orders not only called for him to proceed against Villa and his followers but also directed him to pay scrupulous regard at all times to Mexican sovereignty. In the meantime, newspapers across the United

US CAVALRYMAN AND VILLISTA IRREGULAR

The cavalry corporal from the 10th US Cavalry regiment is wearing a well-worn wool campaign shirt with red and white polka-dot bandanna to protect him from breathing in dust from the desert trails and wind storms. His olive-brown Montana peak campaign hat bears a yellow hat cord designating him to be a cavalryman. His equipment consists of Model 1910 cartridge belt with suspenders of khaki webbing with first-aid pouch suspended from the wearer's right side and bayonet from his left, as well as a M1910 aluminum canteen suspended either from his cartridge belt or to his saddle. His russet brown shoes are strapped with M1911 spurs. He is armed with a Model 1903 Springfield rifle and a M1911 government pistol in a brown leather holster on his right hip, and a Model 1913 Cavalry Saber fitted to his saddle.

The Villista Irregular wore what suited him best in the rough desert terrain of northern Mexico. Popular dress worn by the Villistas consisted of western cowboy/vaquero-style clothing, western cowboy-style boots with large Mexican-style spurs, and a "sombrero" of straw or felt with tricolor ribbon band affixed around the cone of his hat. The ribbon band were in the colors of the Mexican flag and were sometimes marked with "DIVISION DEL NORTE". His kit consisted of a canteen, a haversack made of canvas material bulging with personal rations, a bandolier with 7mm cartridge shells and cartridge belt and holster for his Colt Single Action army revolver with a silver ornate knife tucked into his belt. He is armed with a Colt Single Action army revolver or a Mexican copy thereof as well as a Model 1910 Mauser Rifle.

States, such as *The Santa Fe New Mexican*, announced "President Orders US Army to go Get Pancho Villa Dead or Alive."

On March 14, 1916, Brigadier General John J. Pershing was given command of two cavalry brigades and a brigade of infantry – 10,000 men – with orders to find, pursue, and destroy Villa's forces. The Punitive Expedition advanced into Mexico on March 15, initially with the consent of President Carranza; however, as the expedition wore on through the next 11 months, Carranza became increasingly hostile to it.

On March 15, Pershing's forces crossed the border in two columns with one departing from Columbus and the other from Hachita. Consisting of infantry, cavalry, artillery, engineers, and logistical units, Pershing's command pushed south seeking Villa and established a headquarters at Colonia Dublan near the Casas Grandes River. Though promised use of the Mexican Northwestern Railway, this was not forthcoming and Pershing soon faced a logistical crisis. This was solved by the use of "truck trains," which used Dodge trucks to ferry supplies the 100 miles from Columbus.

Logistically, the Punitive Expedition started as a nightmare. Nothing of this magnitude had ever been attempted by the US Army. Word of the dilemma was forwarded to Secretary of War Newton Baker, who was somehow able to spend $450,000 of unappropriated funds to purchase new trucks. The funds were well spent as more than 10,000 tons of supplies were eventually delivered by truck to Pershing. Moving supplies by truck was no easy feat during the expedition, however, because roads depicted on available

APRIL 12 1916

Battle of Parral

The residence of General John J. Pershing in Fort Bliss, Texas, at the time of the Villista Raid on Columbus, New Mexico, on March 9, 1916. (Photo by the author)

American troops on the march against Villa in Mexico, 1916. (AdeQ Historical Archives)

maps turned out to be nothing but trails that were impassable during wet weather. As a result, engineers had to rebuild many of the roads. The expedition also had to rely on mules and wagons to a large extent to keep supplies moving.

Even though the European armies were already employing thousands of trucks in World War I, the US Army only had about 100 vehicles, located at widely scattered posts and depots throughout the country. On March 14, 1916 the Quartermaster General purchased 54 one-and-a-half-ton trucks from companies in Cleveland, Ohio, and Kenosha, Wisconsin. They left the Great Lakes region on a special southbound freight train on the 16th, and arrived at El Paso on March 18, having covered 1,500 miles in 48 hours, loading and crossing the border into Mexico that same night. From March to July 1916, QM Truck Companies delivered over 4,000 tons of supplies and hundreds of troops to Pershing's mobile force, validating the truck's worth and in the process revolutionizing the US Army's transport.

In addition to the first use of mechanization of transport by the United States Army, aircraft also made their first appearance for the fledgling Army Air Service during the Punitive Expedition. While Villa took the first distinction of utilizing aircraft in combat during the Mexican Revolution, the Americans began experimenting with uses of aircraft as early as 1909 when the army acquired their first Wright Model B. The 1st Aero Squadron, consisting of 11 officers, 84 enlisted men, and a civilian mechanic, moved to Columbus by rail after the Villista Raid. Its first reconnaissance sortie was on March 16. By March 19, 1916 the squadron was assigned to the Punitive Expedition, where it flew into Mexico and operated until February 1917. A forward base was established at Colonia Dublán, the expedition's field headquarters near Nueva Casas Grandes in northern Chihuahua. Detachments continued to serve in Mexico after the squadron returned to Columbus on April 22, 1916, including San

Geronimo, San Antonio, Satevo, Namiquipa, and El Valle, and by the end of May the squadron numbered 16 pilots and 122 enlisted men.

The squadron's Curtiss JN3 airplanes were unable to climb over the 10,000 to 12,000-foot mountains of the region or overcome the high winds of the passes through them. Dust storms frequently grounded the aircraft and wooden propellers delaminated in the heat. The squadron carried mail and dispatches, flew limited reconnaissance, and acted as liaison between Pershing and forward units. By April 20, only two airplanes remained in service (neither flyable, and both were destroyed), four having crashed and two others scavenged to provide replacement parts. Four new Curtiss N8 airplanes were delivered on 22 April, but they were little better than the JN3s

American soldiers guarding the border. Border excursions by armed groups of Mexicans lessened as the Punitive Expedition dispersed the Villistas as a military threat and thousands of soldiers of National Guard units from various states were stationed along the border. (AdeQ Historical Archives)

APRIL 22 1916

7th Cavalry attacks Tomochic

MAY 5, 1916

11th Cavalry attacks Ojos Azules

that they closely resembled and were soon transferred to North Island as trainers. Another Curtiss airplane, the R2, was sent to the 1st Aero Squadron with 12 delivered by late May. The R2 was the latest type available but it too proved unsatisfactory for use on the border. In addition to its Curtiss aircraft, the 1st Aero Squadron also field-tested H-2, H-3, Curtiss Twin JN, R-Land, Sturtevant Advanced Trainer, V-1, D-5, and Curtiss JN-4 during the period 1916–1917. Between March 15 and August 16, 1916, the 1st Aero Squadron flew 540 missions in Mexico.

Dashing south from the Columbus fiasco, Villa struck the mountain village of Namiquipa on March 18, and there defeated the Carranzista garrison of 200 men. Turning to attack Guerrero ten days later, the chubby "centaur" was felled from behind during the fight by a bullet from a .44 Remington rolling block fired by one of his impressed "volunteers." The bullet shattered his shinbone and he was hurriedly evacuated from Guerrero just hours before it was attacked by 370 troopers of the US 7th Cavalry. Led by 63-year-old Colonel George F. Dodd, the 7th charged Guerrero on horses that were completely jaded after a 55-mile march from Bachiniva over the difficult terrain of the Sierra Madre. Villistas poured wildly out of the town in the face of American pistol and rifle fire. Fifty-six guerrillas were killed, and 35 wounded. The 7th reported none killed, five wounded.

On March 29, a patrol of the 7th Cavalry, a detachment of 370 men, attacked Guerrero, believed to be a Villista stronghold. Taken by surprise, the

Columbus had the distinction of having the first tactical military airfield in the United States. A squadron of JN3 Curtis Jennie biplanes provided aerial observation for the expedition, although most of the aircraft were lost to crashes in the rugged Mexican mountains. (Author's photo)

Mexicans were routed from the village; at least 35 Villistas were killed, including Nicolas Hernández, reputedly Villa's right-hand man. While the 7th Cavalry had moved on Guerrero, elements of the 10th Cavalry searched in vain to the east. At Aguas Calientas, on April 1, about 150 Villistas fired on the 10th but were quickly driven off. The American troopers scoured the countryside for fugitives but aborted this operation when they were ordered, on April 10, to advance on Parral, 400 miles south of the border.

Backing up the 7th and 10th Cavalry columns were several smaller "flying columns" assigned to block possible escape routes. When the 13th Cavalry reached Parral just after noon on April 12, 1916, they found the reception far from friendly. Major Tompkins was ushered into the office of General Ismael Lozano, a Constitutionalist officer, who told him that he should never have entered the town and demanded that he leave at once. As Tompkins led his men out of town, they were pursued by a large crowd shouting, "*Viva Villa*" and "*Viva Mexico*." Tompkins drew a laugh by shouting "*Viva Villa*" back at them.

Outside Parral, Carranzista soldiers began firing on the retreating Americans. A sergeant standing next to Tompkins was hit and killed. The major dismounted a rear guard and had them take up position on a small hill. From here they let loose accurate rifle fire, killing an estimated 25 of their pursuers. Then the troopers set off again, until they had to make their next stand, killing another 45 Mexicans. The running battle, during which two

**MAY 14
1916**

Patton's skirmish with Cárdenas

A 1915 Jeffery-Quad Armored Car No. 1 on display at the Pancho Villa State Park, Columbus, New Mexico. At least one Jeffery, along with a White Armored Car and the armored cars from the New York National Guard, was used in the Punitive Expedition against Pancho Villa in 1916. (Author's photo)

Americans were killed and six wounded (including Tompkins), continued late into the afternoon, until the Americans finally marched into the fortified village of Santa Cruz de Villegas, 8 miles from Parral. Although they had found temporary shelter, the situation still looked grim – about 100 American troopers were surrounded by 500 to 600 Carranzistas.

Tompkins sent out scouts to find reinforcements and one of his troopers located a squadron of the 10th Cavalry a few miles away. They had scattered about 150 Villistas in the village of Agua Caliente (not far from Guerrero) on April 1 and had been moving south at a somewhat slower pace. Now Major Charles Young, one of the few black officers in the army, spurred his Buffalo Soldiers toward Santa Cruz. They arrived just before 8p.m. on 12 April.

Though no one knew it at the time, the battle of Parral was a turning point: It marked the Punitive Expedition's furthest penetration into Mexico, 516 miles, and the first time Americans had clashed with Carranzistas. Though there would be more battles to fight, the expedition would now begin a gradual pull-out from Mexico. The squadron withdrew to Santa Cruz de Villegas, and on April 13 was reinforced by elements of the 10th and 11th cavalries. The situation at Parral developed into a standoff between US and Mexican forces that threatened to propel the nations to the verge of war. To avert this, Pershing ordered his troops to withdraw from Parral. Seeking to avoid further provocation, Pershing decided to use his five cavalry regiments to patrol prescribed areas only.

On April 22, while pulling back to its assigned district, the 7th Cavalry encountered Villistas and defeated them at Tomochic. Another of Villa's generals, Candelario Cervantes, who was said to have personally led the attack on Columbus, New Mexico, was killed when he and some of his men stumbled into a gunfight with a small US Army party on a mapping expedition.

On May 5, Major Robert L. Howze led a squadron of the 11th Cavalry against a Villista band at Ojos Azules. In a spectacular fight at a ranch, Howze led his cavalry, supplemented by a machine-gun troop and a contingent of Apache scouts, in a pistol charge. Six troops of that regiment attacked the Villistas. The bugler sounded the charge as the troopers swept through the area and engaged the enemy. The small mules carrying the machine guns and ammunition could not keep up, falling too far behind the charge to allow the guns to be brought into effective range. Despite barbed-wire entanglements that prevented maneuvering of his troops, Howze charged directly at the ranch buildings. Sixty-one bandits were slain, with not one US casualty. This was the "last cavalry charge" distinction given to the 11th US Cavalry in the Mexican Punitive Expedition.

National Guard units from Texas, Arizona, and New Mexico had been called into service on May 8, 1916. With congressional approval of the National Defense Act on June 3, 1916, National Guard units from the remainder of the states and the District of Columbia were also called for duty on the border. In mid-June President Wilson called out 110,000 National Guardsmen for border service. None of the National Guard troops would cross the border into Mexico but were used instead as a show of force.

Nonetheless, activities on the border were far from dull. The troops had to be on constant alert as border raids were still an occasional nuisance.

During Pershing's expedition into Mexico, activities on the border were far from dull. The troops had to be on constant alert as border raids were still an occasional nuisance. Three of the raids were particularly bloody. On May 5, 1916 Mexican bandits attacked an outpost at Glenn Springs, Texas, killing one civilian and wounding three American soldiers. On June 15 bandits killed four American soldiers at San Ygnacio, Texas, and on July 31 one American soldier and a US customs inspector were killed. In all three cases Mexican raiders were killed and wounded, but the exact numbers are unknown. These excursions dwindled as Villa's forces were diminished through attrition with Pershing's relentless pursuit.

Almost left behind at Fort Bliss, 2nd Lieutenant George S. Patton Jr. had wangled an appointment as General Pershing's temporary aide-de-camp. During the Punitive Expedition, Lieutenant Patton was sent out with three headquarters Dodge touring cars, ten soldiers from the Sixth Infantry, two civilian chauffeurs, and two civilian guides to buy corn for the headquarters detachment's horses.

Entering the town a few minutes before noon, one of Patton's guides, an ex-Villista named E.L. Holmdahl, spotted a number of men loitering around the plaza. Although they were unarmed, he recognized some of them as Villistas he had soldiered with in campaigns against Huerta. "They are Villa's men," he whispered, "and they are a bad lot." As the men sighted Holmdahl, they drifted away down the crooked side streets of the town. Holmdahl's warning, however, set off alarm bells in the young lieutenant's mind. Colonel Julio Cárdenas, former leader of Villa's elite troop of "Dorados," was rumored to be in the area.

Hearing in a local Mexican town that a Villista leader might be nearby, the enterprising young officer decided to make a detour to check out the story. His small caravan steered toward the San Miguelito Ranch owned by Villa's most trusted colonel. 2nd Lieutenant George S. Patton and his force, riding in Dodge touring autos, approached the San Miguelito Ranch from the south, appropriately at high noon on May 14, 1916. Patton positioned two carloads – eight soldiers and a guide – at the southern wall around the hacienda and its two gates. He and the remaining two soldiers (a corporal and a private) and a guide parked their car northwest of the compound and made their way east along the low north wall, heading toward the big arch of the main gate.

Patton carried a rifle in his left hand, with his right on the pistol butt at his hip. He was almost at the gate when three horsemen dashed out of the hacienda into the courtyard and headed southeast, running right into the Americans stationed there. The Mexicans immediately wheeled around and charged toward Patton. Bullets whizzed around the lieutenant as he pulled his Colt single-action from its holster and returned fire. One bullet broke the left arm of the lead rider, who was later identified as Coronel Julio Cárdenas, a close aide to Pancho Villa. Another shot took down his horse. The wounded man scrambled for cover as Patton retreated to a wall to reload. The other two Mexican riders split up, trying to escape.

Patton saw one of them go by and shot the horse in the hip, knocking down the mount and the soldier. In an act of chivalry, the American waited for the Mexican to extricate himself, stand up and pull his weapon – only then did Patton (and a couple of his men) shoot and kill him.

The third Villista almost made good his escape, riding hard some 100 yards east of the hacienda. Patton holstered his pistol and aimed his rifle. He and several of his command opened up. The Mexican fell dead in the dust. Meanwhile, in the confusion, Cárdenas had exited on foot through the southwest gate and was running for some fields. Holmdahl caught up with the wounded man, who fell to the ground and put up his good, right arm in a sign of surrender. Holmdahl approached with a drawn revolver to take the Mexican into custody. Cárdenas dropped his hand and pulled his pistol. His shot missed. Holmdahl put a bullet in the colonel's head.

The dead Villistas were later identified as Colonel Cárdenas, Private Juan Garza, and Captain Isadór Lopez. The body of the bandit colonel bore five wounds, and his bandoliers held 35 empty cartridge loops. The two notches on the left ivory grip of the Patton Peacemaker are believed to have been placed there by him to represent the killings of Cárdenas and Garza.

Patton's men tied the bodies to the hoods of the cars, while Patton put Cárdenas' silver-studded saddle and sword into his vehicle. The spectacle of the three cars with the bodies tied on the hoods caused a great commotion along the road, but Patton and his party sped through the countryside to their headquarters at Dublan without incident.

At around 4p.m., Patton arrived at Dublan with the three bloody corpses strapped across the blistering-hot hoods of the automobiles. War correspondents crowded around to get a first-hand account of his adventure. The stories they filed made Patton a national hero for several weeks. His

At the time of the raid the US Army only had about 100 vehicles, located at widely scattered posts and depots throughout the country. On March 14, 1916 the Quartermaster General purchased 54 one-and-a-half ton trucks from companies in the Great Lakes region. They left the region on a special southbound freight train on the 16th, and arrived at El Paso on March 18, having covered 1,500 miles in 48 hours. They loaded and crossed the border into Mexico that same night. (AdeQ Historical Archives)

photograph appeared in newspapers around the United States. Pershing was pleased that someone had enlivened the hunt for Villa and actually taken out a key member of his band. He even permitted Patton to keep Cárdenas' sword and silver saddle as trophies of his first fight. His reward came with a promotion to 1st Lieutenant and Pershing's affectionate description of him as "my bandit."

The battles of April 22 and May 5 were the last "major" engagements of the Punitive Expedition although in minor fights during May two of Villa's principal commanders, Julio Cárdenas and Candelario Cervantes, were killed. In the meantime, however, relations between the United States and the Carranza government deteriorated further as Mexican bands continued to raid US border towns along the lower Rio Grande. A number of the raids had been led by Carranzistas, rather than Villistas. It was at this point, with the National Guard mobilized, that US troop strength along the border reached six figures. On the Mexican side of the border a severe fight broke out in Carrizal at the end of June when a 10th Cavalry patrol entered the town without Carranzista permission.

By May 19, 1916, the 10th Cavalry was in camp at Colonia Dublan alongside the 11th Cavalry. Here they would spend the remainder of their time in Mexico, with periodic scouting expeditions. The planes of the 1st Aero Squadron were out of commission, either wrecked or broken down, and could not be used for reconnaissance. So the job of scouting fell to the cavalry. One such scouting expedition was sent out on June 16 to check on the Mexican troop build-up around Ahumada. Captain Charles T. Boyd, in command of C Troop, with Hank Adair as his lieutenant, was given orders to recon in the vicinity of the Santa Domingo Ranch and to avoid any clash

Despite the mechanized nature of the expedition the bulk of the army were still powered by horses and mules as evidenced by these wagons. Of interest is the cover of one wagon stenciled with "SANITARY TRAIN 6 ART / U.S." on the side. (AdeQ Historical Archives)

THE BATTLE OF CARRIZAL, CHIHUAHUA

JUNE 21, 1916

A veteran recounted the action at Carrizal:

We started forward deployed in line of foragers, moved forward until we were within 500 yards of the enemy, then we dismounted and our horses moved to the rear and we moved forward, the Mexican cavalry started riding around both flanks and when we were about 200 yards from the enemy, we received a heavy volume of fire from rifle and machine guns and we knew that the ball was opened then.

We then received the order to lie down and commence firing, using the battle sight (which is the way we aim our rifles when we are fighting at close range). All of our men were taking careful aim, and Mexicans and horses were falling in all directions but the Mexican forces were too strong for us as they had between 400 and 500 and we only had 50 men on the firing line, so even though we were inflicting terrible execution, they outnumbered us too greatly for us to stop their advance around our right flank.

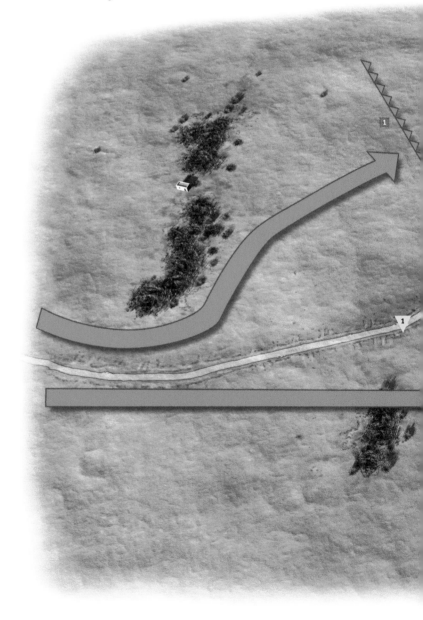

At this stage of the game, the Mexicans were so close that it was almost impossible to miss them, they were even so close that it was possible to hit them with stones had we desired. After about 1½ hours hard fighting they were about 30 yards from our right flank. I tried to swing the left half of our platoon (of which I was in command) around so as to help out our platoon on the right, but it was impossible, about that time our Captain yelled out to Sergeant Page, Quote, "Sergeant Page! Good God man, there they are right upon you!" and Sergeant Page responded, "I see them Captain but we can't stop them and we can't stay here because it is getting too hot". By that time bullets were falling like rain and the Captain ordered all of us to look out for ourselves and our men moved off the field by our left flank. No one can truthfully say that our men ran off the field because they did not, in fact they walked off the field stopping and firing at intervals.

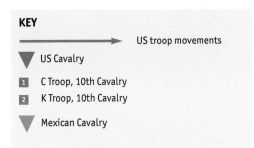

KEY

→ US troop movements

▼ US Cavalry

[1] C Troop, 10th Cavalry

[2] K Troop, 10th Cavalry

▼ Mexican Cavalry

▼ EVENTS

1 Conference between US and Mexican forces

2 Captain Charles T. Boyd falls

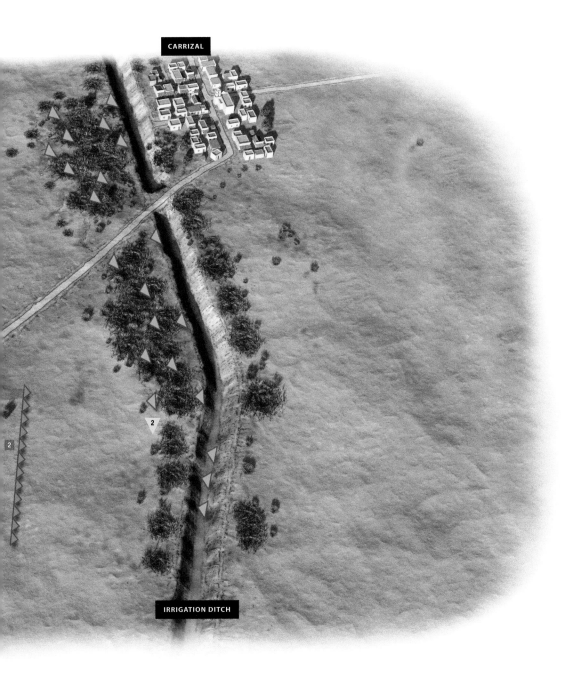

CARRIZAL

IRRIGATION DITCH

SOLDADOS DEL 10 REG DE CAB. NORTEAMERICANO HECHOS PRICIONEROS EN EL COMBATE DEL CARRIZAL POR TROPAS CONST DE MEXICO EL 21 DE JUNIO. DE 1916.

10th Cavalry troopers along with their scout Lem Spillsbury captured by Carranzista troops after the battle of Carrizal, Mexico. Return of the prisoners occurred on June 21, 1916 on the International Bridge at El Paso, Texas. (AdeQ Historical Archives)

with Mexican forces. Similar orders were issued to Captain Lewis S. Morey, Troop K. Captain George B. Rodney watched as Boyd's troop left camp and he counted the men as they rode past. "… Sixty-four men in column, joking and laughing as they filed out of camp; then his 'point' of four men shot to the front and he and Adair waved their hands to me in laughing adieu."[18]

The two columns converged on the ranch, about 60 miles east of Colonia Dublan, on the evening of June 20. There they gathered intelligence on Mexican troops at Ahumada from the American foreman, but Boyd felt that his orders required him to take a look for himself. So the two troops left at dawn on the 21st for Ahumada via Carrizal. Just outside of the town of Carrizal, Boyd found a Mexican government force, estimated at "several hundred" in battle position, awaiting his detachment. They were deployed behind a row of cottonwoods along a stream bed, and in the town, which was fronted by a barbed-wire fence. Between Boyd and the Mexican defenses was an irrigation ditch filled with water. The Mexican commander and his entourage met him and informed Boyd that his orders were to prevent the Americans from advancing any further to the east. Boyd replied that his orders required him to pass through the town.

A long discussion ensued, with the Mexicans opposing the entry of the troops and the American commander insisting on his orders. It is reported that finally the Mexican commander offered to allow the two troops to pass through the town in column of fours, but fearing a trap this was

18 Rodney, p.276

declined. At any rate the discussion was closed by the Mexican returning to the town and the prompt disposition for attack by the two troops, whose combined strength was less than 80 men. The led horses were sent to the rear and troops were formed in line of skirmishers, Troop K being well to the right, with orders to protect the right flank. With this disposition the line moved forward.

As the line drew closer to the edge of the mesa where a barbed-wire fence edged the creek, fire was opened on them from two machine guns that the Mexicans had cleverly disposed under cover. The fire was returned, but the machine-gun fire had already played havoc with the horses, stampeding several of them. C Troop, charging forward, lost Captain Boyd, who was shot first in the hand, then in the shoulder, and then as he sprang out of the irrigation ditch to lead his men he was shot in the head and died instantly. Lieutenant Adair took the troop and carried it forward, storming the town. The two machine guns had previously been put out of action by the hot fire from Troop C. At this stage of the fight Troop K, on the right flank, came under a heavy flanking fire from some Mexican soldiers in a cottonwood grove, and a party of Mexican cavalry appearing at the moment on the right flank of Troop K, that troop fell back, leaving the right flank of Troop C exposed to the hostile fire. Lieutenant Adair, having advanced to the line of houses in the town, found that his men were short of ammunition and went back to get the belts from the wounded, of whom there were quite a few. As he came back he was shot while crossing the irrigation ditch. The bullet struck him just above the heart and he died a few minutes later. With no officers left in the troop, the men became confused. Realizing that they were opposed by tremendous odds – and that they had no support, for K troop had retired – they retreated, but not until they had inflicted a loss of about 80 on the enemy, including their commanding general.

The horses of both troops, stampeded by the bullets that went into the herds, did not stop till they came to the San Domingo ranch where the men found them later. The two troops, losing all cohesion, dropped back to the ranch and got the horses. Both Troop C officers and six enlisted men were killed, four others wounded, and eight were taken prisoner. K Troop lost four enlisted men, Captain Morey and six men wounded, and 15 enlisted men taken prisoner. Lieutenant Adair, along with Captain Charles T. Boyd, was killed by Carranzista troops at Carrizal, Chihuahua, on June 21, 1916. Streets at either end of Fort Huachuca parade ground are named for these two officers. General Pershing officially mourned the loss of Captain Boyd and Lieutenant Adair. "The memory of the splendid bravery of these two officers, who lost their lives, and of the men who personally followed them is cherished by this entire command." All the prisoners captured by the Carranzista troops were returned to US custody ten days later at El Paso, Texas.

The Mexicans lost their commander, General Felix U. Gomez, and 11 other officers. Thirty-three of their enlisted were killed and 53 others wounded. They were disorganized enough to lose their advantage and many of the American troopers avoided capture by escaping on foot into the countryside to be picked up later by rescuing troops.

A Carranzista Cavalry unit during the Mexican Revolution. This image was taken at the time of the funeral for President Carranza. (AdeQ Historical Archives)

JUNE 21, 1916

Battle of Carrizal

Tensions between the United States and Mexico were at a breaking point. Not since the Mexican–American War of 1846–48 had the two countries come so close to all-out war. Neither country was prepared, and neither wanted war. The War Department recognized that a force of at least 200,000 was needed to invade Mexico and that Carranza did not have the troops to ward off an American invasion. To avoid further incidents like Carrizal, Funston ordered Pershing to cease sending out long-range patrols. It was becoming increasingly obvious that Carranza's de facto government openly disliked the American presence in Mexico. Major General Hugh Scott and Funston met with Carranza's military chief, Álvaro Obregón, at El Paso and agreed to gradually withdraw Pershing's forces if Carranza would control Villa.

The expedition learned that some of Carranza's soldiers were joining forces with the Villistas. To counter this threat, Pershing's men spent the remainder of their time operating in a limited area close to their base of operations at Dublan. By order of General Funston, the supply route was moved further north to prevent Carranza's men from cutting off the expeditionary force from Columbus. It was not really necessary for Pershing to send troops any further into Mexico. Villa's forces at this point were badly depleted by casualties and desertion, and those who remained were widely scattered. Although the Villistas were still on the loose, they were not much of a menace.

In September the indefatigable Pancho, his wound healed, surfaced and attacked Satevó and Santa Isabél, killing hundreds of Carranzistas. Gathering followers, he looted Chihuahua on September 16 and "persuaded" 1000 Carranzistas to enlist in his army. Rapid successes at Parral, Correón, and Camargo followed. On Thanksgiving Day, Villa reoccupied Chihuahua and picked up 2000 more Constitutionalist converts.

Pershing, furious at Wilson's orders that he avoid conflict with Carranzista forces and push no further into Mexico, pleaded to be allowed to take Chihuahua and put Villa out of commission once and for all. Anxious to avoid a war with Carranza's government that would entangle his army in Mexico and leave the US prey to smoldering plots of Germany, Wilson held back the indignant Pershing. In January 1917 the problem resolved itself when Villa received his final trouncing by Federalists near Torreón.

The focus of the Punitive Expedition now changed from actively seeking out Pancho Villa to a more defensive position of protecting the troops from

Pershing's Punitive
Expedition into Mexico,
1916–1917

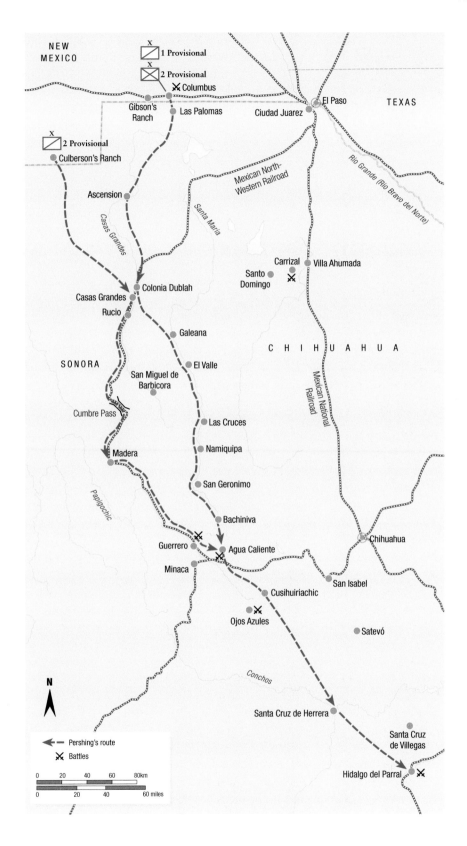

Members of the 6th Field Artillery Regiment preparing their guns as infantrymen march past in the distance. (AdeQ Historical Archives)

Carranza's forces. A new enemy, boredom, now tormented the troops. During the warmer months, they faced an almost daily dose of dust storms and swarms of flies. Organized recreation was virtually nonexistent for the men on duty in Mexico. In the absence of a USO or YMCA, soldiers organized baseball games, boxing matches, and hunting expeditions. Gambling was also another diversion for the troops, since they had nowhere to spend their army pay. As long as no disorder resulted from the gambling, Pershing and his staff made little effort to discourage it.

Another feature of the camp at Colonia Dublan was the numerous Mexican prostitutes who followed the troops. To prevent the men from leaving camp, Pershing had the prostitutes rounded up and placed under guard in a specially created barbed-wire stockade. Soldiers wishing to visit the stockade were required to show the guard on duty that they had the necessary fee, which was regulated by the provost marshal. Before completing business with one of the visiting ladies, a soldier was required to take a prophylactic provided by the army. The result of this strict sanitary measure was one of the lowest venereal disease rates an army has ever known.

The events in Carrizal shocked both sides to the negotiating table. Pershing reduced the scope of his operations, concentrating around his main base at Colonia Dublan. Talks with Carranza petered out but the crisis between the two governments eased. Although Villa remained at large and even organized a new army in southern Mexico, it was the events in Europe in January 1917 that were drawing the United States into World War I, and President Wilson was forced to order the withdrawal of the Punitive Expedition from Mexico.

On January 18, 1917 General Funston informed Pershing "that it was the intention of the Government to withdraw from Mexico at an early date." Pershing "recommended that the date of the beginning of the movement from Dublan, Mexico, be not later than January 28, 1917, the withdrawal to be entirely by marching, and the command to assemble at Palomas, Chihuahua, and march across the border together." The troops marched out of Colonia Dublan on January 30 and recrossed the border at Columbus, New Mexico, on 5 February, 1917. Shortly after the withdrawal, various units of the National Guard were returned to their homes. Small forces were maintained in Texas, Arizona, and New Mexico to "prevent further trouble from scattered bands of outlaws."

The following US Army units were involved in the punitive expedition between 1916 and 1917: 5th, 7th, 10th, 11th, 12th, and 13th Regiments of Cavalry; 6th, 16th, 17th, and 24th Regiments of Infantry; Batteries B and C, 6th Field Artillery; 1st Battalion 4th Field Artillery; Companies E and H, 2nd Battalion of Engineers; Ambulance Company Number 7, Field Hospital Number 7, Signal Corps detachments, 1st Aero Squadron; and Wagon Companies Number 1 and 2. By the end of the Punitive Expedition over 148,000 men served in the expedition and/or along the US and Mexican border.

So the bands were dispersed, and a number of Villa's principal lieutenants were killed: General Hernandez at Guerrero; Pablo Lopez, wounded at Columbus, captured by Carranzistas, and executed in April; Captain Silva killed by Howze at La Joya April 10; Lieutenant Beltran, killed by Howze at Santa Cruz de Herrera April 11; Cervantes, Villa's chief lieutenant in the Columbus fight, killed May 25 by an infantry scouting party; Colonel Cárdenas killed May 14 by Lieutenant Patton. In General Pershing's report of 10 October, 1916 he stated that:

> The number of Villistas who participated in the Columbus Raid based on information received from native sources, is four hundred and eighty-five. The casualty list of Columbus raiders in actions from March 9, to June 30, includes their losses at Columbus. ... Of the total number of 485 Villistas who attacked Columbus, N.M., two hundred seventy three have been reported killed; one hundred eight wounded, who are not captured; nineteen are held in confinement by US troops; and one hundred fifty six are still at large, of whom sixty have been amnestied by the de-facto government, leaving thirty seven unaccounted for.

AFTERMATH

Further Border Incidents

By 1918 the US had declared war on Germany, thus entering World War I. The situation in Mexico had been terrible since the beginning of the revolution in 1910. While fighting the Germans overseas, US forces still had an obligation to defend the United States' southern border. Border excursions did occur after the troops returned to the United States – there were small engagements at Buena Vista, Mexico (December 1, 1917), San Bernardino Canyon, Mexico (December 26, 1917), near La Grulla, Texas (January 8–9, 1918), Pilares, Mexico (March 28, 1918), Nogales, Arizona (August 27, 1918), and near El Paso, Texas (June 15–16, 1919). However, they were not as effective or notable as those that led up to the Columbus raid in 1916 – with the exception of Nogales, where US forces were engaged in combat with a federal Mexican garrison occupying Nogales, Sonora, and a group of German military advisers.

For years, the Yaqui native Americans struggled against Mexico in hopes of establishing an independent state in northern Sonora. In 1918 the fight was still at hand. Yaquis, being poor peasants, would smuggle themselves across the border into Arizona, where they traveled to Tucson to find work in the orange groves. Upon payment, the Yaquis would purchase weapons and return to Mexico to fight their war. In 1917, American farmers and ranchers began reporting sightings of armed native Americans and butchered livestock in their grazing ranges, which prompted the United States Army to conduct border patrols in the area. Yaqui natives had constructed a base in Bear Valley, along trails widely used by travelers passing to and from Mexico. The natives positioned their camp on a ridge inside the valley.

On January 9, 1918 a small force of US 10th Cavalry soldiers detected a band of over two dozen Yaquis hiking up to their camp. At some point the Yaquis discovered the advancing Americans and hastily began to withdraw, leaving behind ten men to protect their retreat. The US Cavalry stopped and then dismounted. The Americans' orders were simple: deny the Yaquis their base by advancing and capturing their camp. Now on foot, the cavalrymen proceeded up to the camp. Once in range, the Yaquis opened fire with

JANUARY 16 1917

Zimmerman Telegram sent

minimal accuracy, as did the Americans. Under fire, the US Cavalry moved forward. For 30 minutes the two forces fought in the classic Indian War style. Both sides relied on natural cover. Eventually the Yaquis surrendered, after their chief was wounded in the chest by a bullet that hit his ammo cartridges, triggering an explosion that left an open wound.

No Americans were killed that day but some were reported to have minor injuries. The Yaquis, one of whom was ten years old, were captured and the US Army gave aid to the wounded natives. On their way back to Nogales, the Yaqui chief died of his injury. The rest of the natives, except for the boy, were taken back and put in jail on charges of gun smuggling and other minor crimes. Some spent a few weeks in jail but were eventually released.

When asked why the Yaquis fired on the approaching Americans, they replied by saying they thought the American buffalo soldiers involved were Mexicans coming to attack them. The small battle marks the last engagement between the United States Army and native Americans, thus ending the American Indian Wars for good.

Throughout the Mexican Revolution US forces garrisoned America's border towns, occasionally exchanging fire with Mexican rebels or federals. With the British interception of the Zimmerman Telegram in 1917, the United States knew well of Germany's attempt to bring Mexico into the war on the side of the Central Powers.

In the beginning of 1918, the US Intelligence Division in southern Arizona began reporting that German agents were teaching the Mexican Army military procedures and building defenses. A few days before the fighting began, an anonymous letter was received by Lieutenant Colonel Frederick J. Herman from someone claiming to be an officer in Pancho Villa's army. In the message, the unknown Mexican warns Herman of the German espionage in and around Nogales, Sonora. The letter also warns of an attack or raid that was to take place somewhere around the end of August. This increased tension along the border. A squad of German military advisers were training the Mexican Army garrison of Nogales, Sonora, and the American troops stationed in southern Arizona were well aware of their operations.

On August 27, 1918, at about 4:10p.m., a gun battle erupted unintentionally when a Mexican civilian attempted to pass through the border, back to Mexico, without being interrogated at the US customs house. The man was suspected of gun smuggling and refused to stop. As he passed the office, customs inspector Arthur G. Barber ordered him to halt. The Mexican failed to halt, leading Inspector Barber to run after him with pistol in hand, followed by two enlisted men. A Mexican officer, on the Mexican side of the border, witnessed the chase, saw Barber with his pistol in hand, drew his own and fired at the customs inspector at or just inside Mexico. The shot missed Barber but hit one of the soldiers, killing him instantly. The other enlisted man then raised his weapon and fired, killing the hostile Mexican officer. After the initial shooting, reinforcements from both sides rushed to the border line. Hostilities quickly escalated.

When the US 35th Infantry garrison of Nogales requested reinforcements, the Buffalo Soldiers of the 10th Cavalry, commanded by Frederick Herman,

JANUARY 18 1917

Pershing informed of planned withdrawal from Mexico

FEBRUARY 5 1917

Pershing's forces cross back into US territory

An American infantryman displaying his equipment consisting of his Model 1903 Springfield Rifle (.30-06 Caliber) and two Model 1911 Government Pistols (.45 ACP). (AdeQ Historical Archives)

came to their aid from their camp outside of town. After observing the situation for a few moments, Lieutenant Colonel Herman ordered an attack south of the border to secure the Mexican hilltops overlooking the Sonoran border town. Defensive trenches and machine-gun placements had been seen being dug on those hilltops during the previous weeks. Herman wanted his forces to occupy the position before Mexican reinforcements got there.

Under heavy fire, the US infantry and dismounted cavalry advanced across the border through the buildings and streets of Nogales, Sonora, and up on to the hilltops. Some armed Arizona citizens tagged along, but most US militia stayed on the American side, firing their weapons from their house windows. Individuals dressed as Mexican civilians and armed with military rifles helped fight the Americans.

About 7:45p.m., the Mexicans waved a large white flag of surrender over their customs building; Lieutenant Colonel Herman then ordered an immediate ceasefire. Snipers on both sides continued shooting for a little while, but were eventually silenced upon orders from their superiors.

Because the battle began as a minor shooting incident and not as a full-scale assault the situation was quickly deescalated. The Americans claimed that the Mexicans and their German advisers were defeated before they could launch their supposed attack or raid into the United States. This was the last hostile action in the border conflict known as the Border War from 1910 to 1918.

The US Army suffered three dead and 29 wounded, of which one died later of wounds. Arizona militia and civilian casualties were two dead and several wounded. According to the US Army, the graves for 129 Mexicans were dug. However, Mexican casualties reported in various newspapers ranged from 30 to 129 dead or wounded in action. The bodies of two German advisers were recovered and examined by the Americans before they were buried. It was reported that other German advisers fled southward. Never again were there reports of Mexican troops massing on the Arizona border or German soldiers and or advisers in the border region. After the battle, German military activity in northern Sonora ceased and the consequences of the incident were settled diplomatically. This was the only land battle fought between Germans and Americans in North America.

One of the last actions taken by the United States Army during the Mexican border conflict occurred when the 24th Infantry stationed in El

Paso took up positions at the Santa Fe Street Bridge on the evening of June 15, 1919. In addition the regiment manned armored machine-gun trucks with crews from the machine gun company. Considerable firing in Juarez was reported by the regiment and several stray bullets struck the Immigration Building where the regimental headquarters were set up. By 3:15a.m. reports were received that all of Juarez, with the exception of Fort Hidalgo, were in possession of the Mexican rebels. By 4a.m. firing resumed in the vicinity of the fort and within 30 minutes the flashes of the rifles advanced within 800 yards of the Santa Fe Bridge. Bullets began falling on the American positions, wounding two soldiers. By 5a.m. federal troops had retaken the positions on the Mexican side of the bridge.

An advance guard from the 24th Infantry crossed into Mexico by 11:45p.m. to face Villista forces near the race track. There the Villistas fired upon members of Companies E and G and the Americans returned fire. One American was wounded and another killed in the encounter. Juarez was retaken and occupied by the 24th until the following day, when the US forces were ordered back across the border. The regiment reported back to Camp Owen Bierne by 11:30a.m. By June 25, 1919 the regiment was moved to Columbus, New Mexico. With the main phase of the Mexican Revolution ending in 1920 further tensions and potential conflict along the Mexican–American border had been reduced.

Convicted Criminals or Prisoners of War?

The morning headlines of the *Albuquerque Journal* on August 28, 1917 told the story in one brief statement: "Seventeen Mexicans in the Columbus Raid Guilty in Second Degree." Previous to the conviction of the 17, four Mexicans who had been captured following the raid were executed by hanging in Deming, New Mexico. The execution took place less than four months after the Villista Raid on Columbus, New Mexico. They were put to death in pairs, with Eusevio Renteria and Taurino Garcia being placed on the scaffold first. Twenty minutes passed before they were pronounced dead. Jose Rangel and Juan Costilla were next, and they died instantly. No evidence was ever introduced in the trial of the four Villistas that connected them directly with the killings in the Columbus raid. However, these four suffered the consequences of Villa's attack with their lives.

Weeks after the raid a punitive expedition led by General John J. Pershing was organized to find Villa and his men. Approximately 19 had been captured, although a few had died while in captivity. Handcuffed, heavily guarded, and still suffering from the wounds inflicted by Pershing's troops, on the day of their conviction 17 Villistas showed the affects of long confinement in the Silver City jail. The men pleaded guilty to the crime of second-degree murder and were sentenced to serve from 70 to 80 years in the penitentiary. District Judge R. R. Ryan of Silver City handed down the sentence. As the men were 25 years of age or more they faced the prospect of life in prison. The life sentence was not widely accepted by the American press or the public; nothing short of the death of Pancho Villa and everyone involved in the raid would appease them.

American soldiers guarding Villistas prisoners during the Punitive Expedition. Many of these prisoners were handed over to law enforcement officials of the state of New Mexico. Their status was later debated: whether they were to be regarded as bandits or as soldiers, thereby granting them a protected status as prisoners of war. (AdeQ Historical Archives)

In this hostile and turbulent atmosphere of vengeance, New Mexico Governor Octaviano A. Larrazolo was presented with a request for the pardon of 15 of the convicted Villistas. The year was 1920 and it was only his second year in office. Governor Larrazolo, Mexican born, Republican, and no stranger to controversy, was determined not to bend before public and political pressure in what he saw as his moral duty to pardon the Villistas. The same man who declared martial law in McKinley and Colfax counties during the coal strike of 1919 prepared an eloquent defense on behalf of the Villistas captured in the Columbus raid.

In reviewing the transcript of the trial, Larrazolo was appalled by the proceedings in the district court case of New Mexico vs. Eusevio Renteria et al., in which the prosecution failed to present any concrete evidence to connect the defendants with the murder of Charles D. Miller, an American victim of the raid. The jury, which consisted of 12 white males, took only 30 minutes of deliberation to arrive at a verdict of guilty of murder in the first degree. It was obvious to Larrazolo that the testimony of the defendants carried little weight in the eyes of the jury. District Attorney J. S. Vaught, in selecting the jurors, asked each man on the panel the following question:

"If it should develop in this case that the state should fail to show that either one of these defendants or all of them fired the fatal shot which killed Mr. Charles D. Miller, but that they were present at the time this man was killed and assisted in his killing by aiding and abetting in the commission of this murder, would you then return a verdict of murder in the first degree?" The answer by each juror was, "Yes, sir!" The second question was, "You would, knowing that it carried the death penalty?" One by one, potential jurors who indicated that they had reservations or were hesitant to answer "yes" to the second question were immediately dismissed. In this way, the jury was selected and the trial began. The opening remarks of J. S. Vaught, quoted here verbatim, set the tone for the trial. "The state in this case expects to prove to you that on the morning of the ninth of March, 1916, one Charles D. Miller was killed at Columbus, and we expect to prove this to you by the admissions made by these defendants. We do not expect to show you that either of the defendants fired the shots that killed Charles D. Miller, or that they were close by the place where Charles D. Miller was killed, but at the time he was killed, they were in that immediate vicinity assisting in the commission of a felony." In other words, the defendants in this case labeled "Villistas" would be convicted and hanged for murder because they were in the town of Columbus on that day.

Several of the defendants testified that they were forced, by the threat of being killed by Villa, to join his forces. Taurino Garcia testified that he was working as a mason when Villa rode up to him on his way to Chihuahua and forced him to join his army. When Garcia resisted, Villa and his men formed a ring around him, beat him severely with a spade and locked him up for six days without food. Upon his release Garcia was turned over to General Beltron for conscription into Villa's army. Villa's orders were to kill any man who refused to serve. Governor Larrazolo was fully aware of the circumstances that brought many of these men to Columbus and their destiny. For this reason and others, he prepared an executive order for the pardon of 15 of the 17 Mexicans convicted on August 17, 1917. He was determined to expiate these men and to save them from the fate suffered previously by their countrymen in Deming.

The defense prepared by Larrazolo on behalf of the Villistas was benevolent as well as legally sound, following logical legal precedents. He began by describing the movement of the troops into Columbus and reviewing the results of the fighting. He placed his emphasis on the acknowledgement that all the men were common soldiers. He recognized "that all of the defendants were in the ranks of the Villa invading columns, and were all subsequently captured in Mexico by our troops, and having been brought into Luna county, New Mexico, were there indicted, charged with the crime of murdering the people that were killed at Columbus at the time of the assault on the morning of March 9, 1916."

Larrazolo asked that consideration be given to the conditions and circumstances under which these men acted: "Were we at peace with the Republic of Mexico or did a state of war exist between the United States and Mexico?" He proceeded to demonstrate that a state of war did actually

The April 24, 1916 edition of the *New York Times* reported: "Pablo Lopez, who commanded the Villa bandits that massacred seventeen Americans at Santa Ysabel, Chihuahua, was captured in a cave a short distance from Santa Ysabel today by a detachment of Carranza soldiers, and is now being taken to Chihuahua City with three of his bandit followers for execution, according to a message from Santa Ysabel received by General Gabriel Gavira at Juarez this afternoon." (AdeQ Historical Archives)

Execution of Pablo Lopez facing the firing squad

exist at the time of the Columbus raid. A battle between the United States and Mexico had taken place in Veracruz on April 21, 1914. Following the fighting, the United States remained in possession of the port and city for approximately seven months. Larrazolo, was quick to acknowledge that no

In the image, handwritten text reads: "W. H. Horne Co. Copyrighted. El Paso, Tex." and "The Body of Pablo H. Lopez."

actual declaration of war was made, but emphasized that a state of war may exist between nations without a formal declaration of war being made from either side. Because the United States and Mexico were in a state of war, the treatment of the Villistas was material within the framework of the law: the men were in fact prisoners of war and should have been treated and dealt with according to the rules of military engagement. More importantly, Larrazolo argued, civil courts had no jurisdiction in the case.

Larrazolo's defense of the Villistas raised several other legal and moral considerations. After personally cross-examining each of the men involved he discovered that most of them were illiterate, that they were laborers, and they were forced into service against their wills. Larrazolo defended their position in this way:

> It is a fact known to the average laymen, and even the most ignorant of us, that under military discipline, the common soldier, known as a private in the ranks, is never told what the objectives of any military movement is, particularly so when engaged in hostilities. The absolute, unconditional, and passive obedience of the common soldier to his superior officers is so generally known, so well established, and so relentlessly enforced, that it has been a theme for the poet, who speaking of this soldier's obedience to superior officers says: 'It is not for him to ask the reason why. It is for him to obey and die.

The governor then proceeded to review the history of the turmoil in Mexico at that time. He strengthened his defense by describing the campaigns of General Francisco Villa, and the revolutions and counter-revolutions in which he was involved. He emphasized that Villa was indeed the commander of an army and had been in command for ten years. The army under his

An image purporting to show the body of Pablo Lopez being displayed by American troops. It is highly unlikely this is of General Lopez and has probably been misidentified. (AdeQ Historical Archives)

control maintained rank and file, enforced military discipline, and appointed trained officers whose orders were to be obeyed. It was the Villistas' duty under military discipline, Larrazolo pointed out, to obey the orders of their superiors. That order, on the morning of March 9 in Columbus, was to fight the enemy.

To bolster his defense, Governor Larrazolo documented several important legal precedents established in the case of Arce et al. vs. State of Texas. A detachment of Mexican troops attacked United States soldiers on the Texas side of the border and in the ensuing battle there were casualties on both sides. Six Mexican soldiers were taken prisoner, indicted, and charged with the crime of killing William Oberlies, a United States soldier. They were tried, convicted of murder in the first degree, and sentenced to death. The case was appealed. The Criminal Court of Appeals for the state of Texas handed down the following summarized opinion:

> From their testimony, a general statement may be made to the effect that these Mexican soldiers were controlled by their officers in command and were obedient to them; that the command was organized under the authority of the Carranza or de facto government of Mexico and was in fact, a military command. By this testimony it seems that in such circumstances, the soldiers must obey the order of their superiors, and failure to do so would subject them to discipline which rates from minor punishment to death, according to the rule which has been violated by those under its authority. When a soldier is ordered to fight, it is his duty to do so. If he deserts under certain circumstances, he may be shot or executed. At least one of the defendants claimed to have been forced to go into battle by his commanding officer. He did not desire to fight, but under the rules of warfare if he deserted, he would be tried and he would be shot, or if he disobeyed orders and failed to engage in the fight he might forfeit his life. If the state courts had jurisdiction of these defendants, we are of the opinion the conviction would be erroneous. In this case, we are of the opinion that this judgment should be reversed, and the cause remanded.

Upon completing his defense of the Villistas, Governor Larrazolo issued an executive order, released on November 17, 1920, containing a statement that granted to each defendant named a complete, unconditional pardon for the crime of murder. A number of negative reactions to the pardon were received by the governor, though some were more favorable, including the support of A.B. Renehan, a prominent attorney and figurehead of the period. In spite of tremendous pressure from many directions to reverse his decision, Governor Larrazolo stood firm. The Villistas were set free, re-arrested, retried for murder, and acquitted by a jury on April 28, 1921. Sixteen freed Villistas were returned to Mexico on April 30, 1921.

LEGACY

As a token of appreciation, the United States Congress approved the issuing of the Mexican Service Badge, then the Mexican Border Service Medal. Eligibility for the Mexican Service Badge, according to War Department General Order 155, December 1917, was authorized by the president for issue "to all officers and enlisted men who are now, or may hereafter be, in the military service ... in Mexico as members of the Vera Cruz expedition ... in Mexico as members of the punitive or other authorized expeditions ... those who participated in an engagement against Mexicans ... and those who were present as members of the Mexican border patrol." Individuals not eligible were authorized by Congress to receive the medal on July 9, 1918. Its purpose was to recognize the National Guardsmen and regular army troops mobilized to patrol the Mexican border between 1916 and 1917.

After prolonged struggles, representatives produced the Mexican Constitution of 1917 – though effective implementation of the social provisions of the 1917 Constitution of Mexico and near cessation of revolutionary activity did not occur until the administration of Lázaro Cárdenas (1934–1940). The revolution is generally considered to have lasted until 1920 with the death of Carranza, although the country continued to have sporadic, but comparatively minor, outbreaks of warfare well into the 1920s. The Cristero War of 1926 to 1929 was the most significant relapse of bloodshed. Total "demographic cost" during the Mexican Revolution 1910–1920 was approximately 2.1 million people.

In 1920 Obregón finally reached an agreement with Villa, who retired from armed fighting. Three years later Villa was assassinated by a group of seven riflemen while traveling in his car in Parral. It is presumed that the assassination was ordered by Obregón, who feared a supposed bid for the presidency by Villa.

The numerous border incidents, including the Columbus Raid, throughout the Mexican Revolution and the lack of resources available for adequate border protection became the primary concern for many American government officials. But World War I had strained resources from the

The Punitive Expedition was a distant memory as the United States shifted its attention toward World War I in Europe. Pershing's career continued on in greatness and eventually he was promoted to the rank of General of the Armies. "Pershing's Crusaders: Following the Flag to France" was an eight-reel picture released by the US Committee on Public Information in 1918 and documented General Pershing and his troops fighting in the trenches of France.

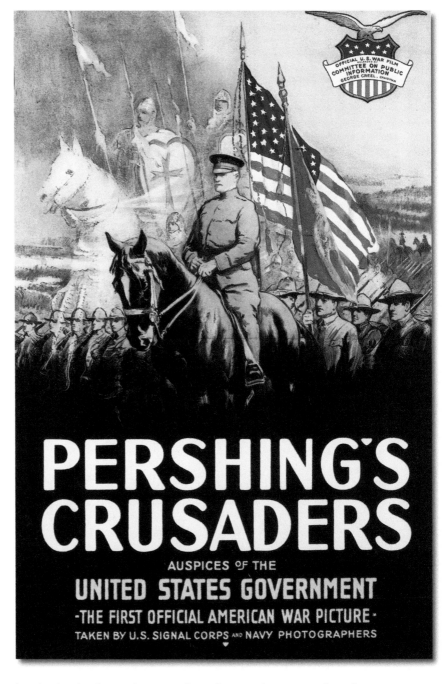

border by the diminishing number of troops being transferred to Europe. In 1918, Supervising Inspector Frank W. Berkshire wrote to the Commissioner-General of Immigration expressing his concerns about the lack of a coordinated, adequate effort to enforce immigration and customs laws along the border with Mexico: "If the services of men now being drafted cannot be spared for this work, it may be that the various departments vitally interested would give favorable consideration to the formation of an independent organization, composed of men with out the draft age. The

assertion is ventured that such an organization, properly equipped and trained, made up of seasoned men, would guard the border more effectively against all forms of lawlessness than a body of soldiers of several times the same number ..."

The Eighteenth Amendment to the United States Constitution, prohibiting the importation, transport, manufacture or sale of alcoholic beverages went into effect at midnight on January 16, 1920. With the passage of this constitutional amendment and the numerical limits placed on immigration to the United States by the Immigration Acts of 1921 and 1924, border enforcement received renewed attention from the government. The numerical limitations resulted in people from around the world trying illegal entry if attempts to enter legally failed. Therefore the mission of the Border Patrol became more important to the US government. These events set the wheels of change into motion. On May 28, 1924 Congress passed the Labor Appropriation Act, officially establishing the US Border Patrol for the purpose of securing the borders between inspection stations. In 1925 its duties were expanded to patrol the sea coast.

Officers were quickly recruited for the new positions and the Border Patrol expanded to 450 officers. Many of the early agents were enlisted from organizations such as the Texas Rangers, local sheriffs and deputies, and appointees from the Civil Service Register of Railroad Mail Clerks. The government initially provided the agents with a badge and revolver; recruits furnished their own horse and saddle, but Washington supplied oats and hay for the horses and a $1,680 annual salary for the agents. The agents did not have uniforms until 1928. Currently at the time of this writing, the United States Border Patrol is a federal law enforcement agency within US Customs and Border Protection (CBP), a component of the Department of Homeland Security (DHS).

Almost overnight Camp Furlong became a large military installation for protection from other raids and for preparation for a Punitive Expedition into Mexico to be led by General Pershing. First on the scene were elements of the New Mexico National Guard. Various regular units then arrived to provide support to the troops in Mexico. The camp also had supply facilities and repair yards for the early motor trucks used in Mexico. At its peak the camp was headquarters for more than 5,000 troops. Following the withdrawal of the Punitive Expedition, the 24th Infantry Regiment was headquartered at the post. With the conclusion of the Mexican Revolution, the post lost its importance and only 100 men were garrisoned there in 1921. All troops in the area were gone by 1923. (Author's photo)

The Battlefield Today

There are still reminders of Pancho Villa's raid on Columbus to this day. Of the buildings still standing are the El Paso & Southwestern Railroad Depot, the school house, Hoover Hotel, and a few other buildings along Broadway Street. The remains of the concrete vault of the Commercial State Bank where Villistas tried breaking in by shooting at the steel vault door can be seen on the corner of Broadway and East Boundary Streets. The steel vault door is preserved and viewed among other relics from the raid at the Columbus Historical Society Museum housed in the former railroad depot. Coote's Hill (now known as Villa Hill) and the remaining portion of Camp Furlong have been preserved.

Pancho Villa State Park was established in 1959 "in interest of preservation of the memory of the unique, historical occasion of the last hostile action by foreign troops within the continental United States" and became the only park in the United States to be named after a foreign invader. The creation of the 60-acre park was a gesture of good will between the United States and Mexico. The town of Columbus has been designated a National Historic Site. At Pancho Villa State Park, several buildings remain from the time of Villa's 1916 raid, and are listed on the National Register of Historic Places. These include the 1902 US customs house, two adobe structures dating from the Camp Furlong-era, the Camp Furlong Recreation Hall and concrete stands for the army truck transports. Pancho Villa State Park's extensive historical exhibits depicting the raid and the US Army's subsequent Punitive Expedition into Mexico are housed in the park's new $1.8 million 7,000-square-foot Exhibit Hall.

Through donations and funds appropriated by the New Mexico Legislature in 1999, Pancho Villa State Park acquired expedition-era examples of the vehicles and technology employed by Pershing and his men. The Exhibit Hall contains a full-size replica Curtiss JN-3 "Jenny" airplane used by the 1st Aero Squadron; a 1916 Dodge touring car, the type used by Pershing for a field office; historic artifacts; military weapons and ribbons. An armored tank stands as a sentinel outside the facility.

On the outskirts of town is the Valley Heights Cemetery where some of the civilian victims of the raid were laid to rest. Among the victims buried there is Bessie (Bain) James and her unborn child. In addition, there is the grave of Henry Arthur McKinney who was killed by Villistas two days before the Columbus raid in Mexico on the ranch of the Palomas Land and Cattle Company. It is the most solemn of the sites related to the raid.

CONCLUSION

One popular explanation among historians regarding Villa's motivation for attacking Columbus is that the Villistas raided the town in search of supplies. The 13th Cavalry stationed at Columbus had precisely the resources Villa needed for his ravaged army. He desperately required machine guns, rifles, and ammunition, and there was an ample supply available within the garrison. The military camp and the town's general stores contained food, clothing, and other provisions vital to Villa's survival as well.

This theory contended that Villa did not vengefully descend upon Columbus, but rather focused on obtaining resources unavailable to him elsewhere. The assertion is that if Villa's intentions were to massacre Americans he would have inflicted many more fatalities during the attack. In fact, only 18 Americans were killed during the affair because the Villistas focused the majority of their efforts on acquiring much-needed supplies. The Villistas especially ignored non-combatants, concentrating mainly on the hotels, whose guests were robbed of their money and valuables, and on stores that were well stocked. Single residences were largely disregarded, especially the homes of Mexican-American citizens, who were judged to be not fit for looting. The Villistas were more concerned with stealing horses and acquiring accessible arms and ammunition. Unfortunately for them, the majority of the arms and ammunitions were locked up or well guarded.

In conclusion, the raid on Columbus by Pancho Villa and the subsequent Punitive Expedition by General Pershing were classic examples of cause and effect without a desired result coming to fruition from either side – an event that similarly occurs in other conflicts in the 20th and 21st centuries since the Columbus Raid such as Somalia in the 1990s and the War on Terror in Afghanistan since the terrorist attacks on 9/11 in 2001. Of these, the latter campaign is probably the best example of what is perceived by the public as a campaign "to get Bin Laden," a feat that has been achieved, as well as the combined allied military achievements in diminishing considerably Al-Qaeda's and the Taliban's power as fighting forces in the region. Regardless of whether Bin Laden had or not had been captured or killed, the campaign in

A composite of images from items of the Fort Bliss Museum consisting of General Pershing's riding crop and command car used during the Punitive Expedition. (Photos by author)

Afghanistan and later in Iraq had considerably destroyed Al-Qaeda's cohesion as an international terrorist organization in the years prior to the 2011 raid in Abbottabad, Pakistan, that finally killed Osama Bin Laden.

Looking at Pershing's Punitive Expedition from a military standpoint, the United States greatly diminished Pancho Villa's role as a threat. After the raid, General Villa was never able to rebuild his army to what it was, he had lost his veteran senior officers and men through attrition, valuable supplies were captured or destroyed, and his political influence was lost. Regardless of the intervention, the loss of the battle of Celaya meant the rise to power of Venustiano Carranza and the Sonora generals.

On the other hand, the young men and officers of the United States Army gained valuable combat and logistical experiences that eventually prepared them for World War I. Additionally, Pershing's forces were experienced in counter-guerrilla warfare and they succeeded in their goal of breaking up and neutralizing the forces that Villa was using to launch raids. By definition a punitive expedition is a military campaign that has officially the goal to punish the failure of the country to which it applies. In short, Pershing's original goal in destroying Villa's force as a threat to the United States had been achieved.

BIBLIOGRAPHY

"American Army Crosses Into Mexico," *Santa Fe New Mexican*, Vol. 53, No. 18, (March 15, 1916), p. 1

Bishop, Dennis, "Pershing Rides: The US Campaign in Mexico, 1916–17," *Strategy & Tactics*, No. 242 (May 2007), pp. 6–18

"Border Fiasco Pathetic Proof of Unreadiness of US Army," *Santa Fe New Mexican*, Vol. 53, No. 21 (March 18, 1916), p. 1

Boucher, Leonard H. "Pancho Villa's Revenge," *True Frontier* (May 1970), pp. 8–12, 51–55

Chalkley, John F., *Zach Lamar Cobb: El Paso Collector of Customs and Intelligence During the Mexican Revolution, 1913–1918*, Texas Western Press/The University of Texas, El Paso, TX (1998)

de Quesada, Alejandro M. and Jowett, Phillip, *The Mexican Revolution 1910–1920*, Osprey Publishing, Oxford (2006)

Deac, Wilfred P., "Manhunt for Pancho Villa," *Military History*, Vol. 19, No. 5 (December 2002), pp. 50–56, 90, 93

Dean, Richard R., *The Columbus Story*, Columbus Historical Society, Inc. Columbus, NM (1994)

Evans, Marie, "Six Hanged for Villa Raid," *The Great Western Historian*, No. 2 (spring 1990), pp. 40–44.

Gault, Jeff, *The Buffalo Soldiers at Fort Bliss, Texas*, Springfield, VA, Army Scholarship Foundation Press (2009)

Griensen, Armando Camacho, *Elisa Griensen y la nueva Expedición Punitiva en Parral: Un pueblo, unos niños y una mujer, Parralenses Desafían al poderoso ejercito Norteamericano*. Chihuahua, Mexico, (2001)

A fanciful depiction of Generals Pershing and Villa shaking hands in friendship in a square in Palomas, Mexico – just across the border from Columbus, NM. The bronze statues are more a symbolic meaning for the two communities that bore the brunt of the Mexican Revolution, Villista Raids, and the Punitive Expedition. (Author's photo)

The railroad depot of the El Paso & Southwestern Railroad in Columbus is one of the few surviving structures from the raid. It is now a historical museum. (Photo by the author)

Habermeyer, Christopher Lance, *Gringos' Curve: Pancho Villa's Massacre of American Miners in Mexico, 1916*, Book Publishers of El Paso, El Paso, TX (2004)

Harris, Charles and Sadler, Louis R., *The Secret War in El Paso: Mexican Revolutionary Intrigue, 1906–1920*, University of New Mexico Press, Albuquerque, NM (2009)

Harris, Larry A., *Pancho Villa And The Pancho Villa Raid*, Superior Printing, Inc., El Paso, TX (1949)

Harris, Larry A., *Pancho Villa: Strong Man of the Revolution*, High-Lonesome Books, Silver City, NM (1989)

Howe, Jerome W., "Campaigning in Mexico, 1916," *Journal of Arizona History*, Part 1, Autumn 1966; Part 2, Winter 1966

Hurst, James W., *Pancho Villa and Black Jack Pershing: The Punitive Expedition in Mexico*, Praeger Publishers, Westport, CT (2008)

Hurst, James W., *The Villista Prisoners of 1916–1917*, Yucca Tree Press, Las Cruces, NM (2000)

Katz, Frederick, *The Life and Times of Pancho Villa*, Stanford University Press, Stanford, CT (1998)

Krauze, Enrique, *Entre el ángel y el fierro: Francisco Villa*, Fondo de Cultura Economómica, Mexico City (1987)

Machado, William C., *Uniforms & Equipment of the Last Campaign, 1916: The Pursuit of Pancho Villa*, Kengraphics Printing & Litho, Ontario, CA (1993)

Mason, Herbert Molloy, *The Great Pursuit: General John J. Pershing's Punitive Expedition across the Rio Grande to destroy the Mexican bandit Pancho Villa*, Random House, New York (1970)

Meed, Douglas V., *Bloody Border: Riots, Battles and Adventure Along the Turbulent US–Mexican Borderlands*, Westernlore Press, Tucson, AZ (1992)

Muller, William G., *The Twenty-Fourth Infantry*, The Old Army Press, Fort Collins, CO (1972)

Pershing, John J., Major General (US Army), REPORT OF THE PUNITIVE EXPEDITION. Report Written in Colonia Dublan, Mexico on October 10, 1916. Copy found in the Library of the Army War College, Carlisle Barracks, PA.

"President Orders US Army to go Get Pancho Villa Dead or Alive," *Santa Fe New Mexican*, Vol. 53, No. 14 (March 10, 1916), p. 1

Rakocy, Bill, *Villa Raids Columbus*, N. Mex., Bravo Press, El Paso, TX (1981)

Rodney, George B., *As a Cavalryman Remembers*, Caxton Printers, Caldwell, Idaho (1944)

Romo, David Dorado, *Ringside Seat to a Revolution – An Underground Cultural History of El Paso and Juárez: 1893–1923*, Cinco Puntos Press, El Paso, TX (2005)

Scott, Hugh B., *Some Memories of a Soldier*, Century Company, New York (1928)

Stivison, Dr. Roy Edward, "Night of Terror," *Old West*, Vol. 10, No. 4 (Summer 1974), pp. 36–37, 41–44

Stout, Joseph A., *Border Conflict: Villistas, Carranzistas and the Punitive Expedition, 1915–1920*, Texas Christian University Press, Fort Worth, TX (1999)

Tompkins, Frank, Colonel (US Army), *Chasing Villa: The Last Campaign of the US Cavalry*, Military Service Publishing Company, Harrisburg, PA (1934)

"Villa Invades the US: Bandits Burn and Kill in Columbus," *Santa Fe New Mexican*, Vol. 53, No. 13, (March 9, 1916), p. 1

"Villa Plot to Invade US Hatched Several Months Since," *Santa Fe New Mexican*, Vol. 53, No. 14 (March 10, 1916), p. 1

INDEX